# How Do They Know That?

# How Do They Know That?

## The Process of Social Research

# MICHAEL V. ANGROSINO

*University of South Florida*

**WAVELAND**

**PRESS, INC.**

Long Grove, Illinois

For information about this book, contact:
Waveland Press, Inc.
4180 IL Route 83, Suite 101
Long Grove, IL  60047-9580
(847) 634-0081
info@waveland.com
www.waveland.com

*To all the chaplains*
*who make caring an everyday reality*
*in the modern hospital*

# Contents

———◆◆◆———

# Acknowledgments

———◆◆◆———

I gratefully acknowledge the willingness of my students in cultural anthropology and sociology at the University of South Florida, the College of New Jersey, and Mercer County Community College, who were willing and enthusiastic participants as I developed the strategy for teaching the fundamentals of the social research process embodied in this book. Their interesting and insightful responses to my challenge to think about "How do they know that?" informs the product you are about to read.

Once again I thank Tom Curtin, Jeni Ogilvie, and their associates at Waveland Press, who have been unfailingly helpful and supportive of my efforts over the years.

# Introduction

# Doing Social Research

Social research is the work of cultural anthropologists, sociologists, social psychologists, and some geographers, economists, and students of education, business, and public health. It is carefully organized inquiry that helps us discover the ways in which human groups work and how individuals and groups influence one another. The conclusions of social research can sometimes seem obvious (e.g., people with good health insurance get better preventive care than those without), but that does not mean that they are the products of everyday intuition. Many conclusions that we now take for granted as simple common sense (e.g., that racial prejudice in the United States has historically led to disparities in education and health care) would have been considered outrageous, or even deliberately inflammatory, just a few decades ago. Other generalizations with wide popular support (e.g., that the "traditional" family consists of a married man and woman and their biologically and/or legally adopted children) turn out to be less than compatible with the empirical evidence. Organized inquiry helps us get past our adherence to the "received wisdom" so that we can engage in a serious interrogation of what we think is self-evidently true.

## Social Research: Basic Premises

Research is the process that leads us away from the too-easy generalizations, from the reliance on naïve common sense, and from the conviction that we already know all we need to know about human behavior simply because of our lived experiences. Sometimes research confirms

1

our received wisdom; more often than not it challenges us to reconsider what we think we know about ourselves and others and the communities in which we live.

I always tell students in my introductory courses that whenever I as a lecturer state something as a fact, or whenever something is presented as a settled conclusion in the textbook, they should ask, "How do they know that?" In effect, I ask them to imagine the process of inquiry that has established a conclusion as somehow factual. Students are usually eager to do so if the conclusion seems counterintuitive. They may be surprised, for example, that the textbook claims that gender is a social category not always the same as biological sex, since this statement seems to fly in the face of observed reality. They therefore are interested in finding out what kind of research could have led to such a finding. But students should ask the same question even if the conclusion seems to fall into the "everybody knows that" category. It may well be that "everyone agrees that this is true" (and the eminent and highly respected professor is among that crowd of "everyone"), but scientific knowledge is not enhanced when we uncritically accept what "everyone" knows; it is important to understand how a proposition came to be established as trustworthy in the first place.

Beginning students tend to have a ready answer to my question. "How do they know that?" Why, "they" asked questions, of course. "They" took a survey. Everyone is familiar with polls, which seem to dominate our everyday news coverage. It sometimes seems as if there is no issue so complex that it cannot be reduced to a few poll numbers. There is a certain truth to this quick answer, but I want my students to probe more deeply. Who were the shadowy "they" who asked questions? What questions did their survey contain? To whom were those questions asked and under what circumstances were they asked? Perhaps most important of all: why was the matter considered worth exploring to begin with? If an issue has a broad and complex social history (such as the problem of racial prejudice) or if it touches on matters that are deeply personal (such as the question of gender and sex), can we rely on simple, direct observations or straightforward questions? Can we always assume that people will tell a surveyor/pollster the unvarnished truth, particularly about sensitive matters? "Taking a survey" is not simply a matter of posing a few questions to whoever happens to be handy, nor is it inevitably the best way to conduct social research. So how do we construct a logical process of inquiry that will lead us from an initial curiosity about some social issue to a conclusion that will be widely seen as satisfying?

Social research is certainly grounded in the two basic operations alluded to in my students' top-of-the-head response: observation and interviewing. But the trick is in using these operations to maximum effect, in deploying them in such a way that they will indeed yield answers that come to be taken as valid and reliable. Research is best thought of as a *process* that takes things we do almost instinctively (observe the world around us and ask questions when necessary) and gives them a logical organization so that they can be replicated and so that the responses can be understood as more than snap judgments or the unreflective repetition of received wisdom.

Beginning students, however, are quick to assume that the research process is something reserved for those more advanced. They are all too often content to assume that "the professor must know what he's talking about," so that my request that they question the sources of my supposed knowledge seems unnecessary, almost perverse. It is my contention, however, that an understanding of the research process is *not* beyond the capabilities of novice students of the social sciences; in fact it is an absolutely essential component of their learning process.

We live in a world of information overload. It is no accident that the Internet is often referred to as the "information superhighway," and not the "knowledge superhighway," much less the "wisdom superhighway." We can easily drown in a sea of undifferentiated data. Not everyone needs to become a professional researcher, but I believe that everyone needs to know how research is conducted so that they can be intelligent consumers of all that information. "How do they know that?" should be the guiding question, not just in the classroom, but also when confronted by one's news source(s) of choice or by the claims of advertisers or politicians. If you cannot see how a particular piece of data came to be known and how it logically articulates into a meaningful pattern with other data, then you need to consider whether it is a valid claim at all.

This book is therefore designed to instill a healthy intellectual skepticism in its readers. My aim is to present the process of social research in a guided, step-by-step fashion so that you, the reader, can see how to organize a process of inquiry that results in the most valid, reliable, and usable conclusions. The material is presented in such a way that even a beginning student can use it as a guide to conceive and carry out a piece of research, for nothing builds an awareness of an abstract process so well as actually doing it for oneself. Throughout the book I illustrate the process with a research project of my own—not because I think it is especially noteworthy in and of itself, but because I can discuss it in detail from beginning to end. Most research reports are of necessity concerned with the author's findings and with only those aspects of the research process that have the most direct bearing on the generation of those conclusions. They are typically rather sketchy when it comes to explications of the complete A through Z of their methods, on the assumption that a professional scholarly audience will be able to fill in the blanks—not much help to someone just learning the ropes.

# Getting Started

It bears noting at the outset that in the typical research process each step requires making critical decisions about how to proceed. There is never a single path through this particular forest. I do not expect you to accept all of my decisions as if they were written in stone—they are simply the ones that seemed to serve the needs of the project I have selected to illustrate the process, for reasons that I endeavor to explain as we go along. I do my best to point out alternative decisions that I could have made that would have yielded different (albeit equally useful) results. In this guide, I use a fairly standard eight-step model for the research process, but there may be as many different ways to navigate those eight steps as there are researchers who want to find out "How do they know that?" The point is that you should reach the end of this book knowing about some of the ways to get from the starting line to the finish—to realize that inquiry is a process in which critical decisions are made at every step of a logically integrated structure.

Handbooks of social research methodology abound, although many of them are too complexly detailed, too focused on the how-to's of specific means of data collection to be of much use to the beginner. This book, by contrast, focuses on the eight-step process itself and the kinds of choices that must be made at each step. You, the reader should come away with an awareness of the logical connections that link the process together and that make it as useful as possible both for the professional researcher and for the intelligent consumer of research data.

When we think of scientific research, we probably first imagine that some sort of experiment is being conducted. Indeed, classic scientific inquiry has been based on carefully controlled experiments designed to test clearly formulated hypotheses. The essence of the experimental research design is the ability of the researcher to control all the variables involved in the problem and to eliminate any extraneous factors that might unexpectedly change the results. When it comes to research into human behavior, however, this classic design can be difficult to achieve. Certain types of individual responses can be tested under laboratory or other controlled situations, but the sorts of activities that take place in groups in natural social settings are rarely, if ever, controllable. Social researchers must therefore make do with designs that are perhaps less elegant but that are more adaptable to the somewhat messy "real world" conditions of primary interest to social researchers.

Social research must be as careful and detailed in its preparation and execution as experimental research; the crucial difference is in the relative lack of control that the researcher exercises over the study participants and their actions. Scientific rigor enters social research through the logical integration of the steps in the process of inquiry rather than through the researcher's absolute control over the conditions of the study. There are two main ways in which the steps of the inquiry process are integrated: the quantitative and the qualitative. These two branches of the social research process may be referred to as the fundamental *paradigms* of scientific inquiry.

# Two Paradigms: A Comparison

Quantitative research (also referred to as "positivist" or "empiricist" research) dominated social science from its beginnings in the mid-nineteenth century to the 1960s; the prevailing view among social scientists was that quantitative research, grounded as it is in statistical analysis of empirical data, was the more nearly "scientific" form of research, the one that more closely approximated the elegant formalism of the experimental design. Qualitative approaches, by contrast, had always been around, particularly among cultural anthropologists; but they gradually came to the fore as a reaction against positivistic assumptions. This is, qualitative researchers questioned the empirical nature of the supposed "facts" that are involved in social issues. Is "racism," for example, a "fact" on a par with "noise levels in a controlled laboratory environment measured by decibel level" or is it a complex inference, a convenient term that covers a multiplicity of attitudes, emotions, and behaviors? If it is the latter, then the attempt to translate the study of racism (or any other complex social issue) into neatly controlled hypothesis tests amenable to statistical analysis must necessarily fail.

As the reader will see, my own preference is for the qualitative forms of research, and I trust that I will make it clear why I favor this approach. But the quantitative and qualitative research paradigms are usefully thought of as tools—that is, as means to an end—rather than ends in and of themselves. A screwdriver is a perfectly good tool—but not if what you need to do is clean your ears. A Q-tip is not "better" than a screwdriver in a universal sense, just in terms of one particular task. So qualitative research is not better than quantitative research—or vice versa; one is just better suited than the other for particular kinds of research. A well-trained social researcher will be familiar with and comfortable using both types of research; the trick is always to decide which one best helps you answer the question at hand. Because I enjoy using qualitative methods more than I do quantitative ones, I have learned to choose research projects that seem to be most efficiently dealt with by those methods. Throughout this book, however, I attempt to show how quantitative methods might have been employed, despite my own option for the qualitative.

It may be helpful at the outset to outline some of the basic differences between the quantitative and the qualitative paradigms of social research. The first issue that divides them is the one alluded to above: what is the nature of reality? Philosophers refer to this as an "ontological question." Quantitative research is based on the assumption that reality is objective—that there is truth "out there" that is independent of anything the researcher might do. It is therefore the job of the researcher to "discover" that truth. Quantitative researchers believe that social reality is grounded in objective "facts"; it is therefore "singular"—there is one right (or, at least, one best) answer to a question. Qualitative researchers, by contrast, treat reality as subjective; it exists essentially as a projection of the consciousness of those who participate in an activity—including the researcher, particularly if he or she becomes an active member of the group being studied. As a result, truth for the qualitative researcher can be "multiple"—there may be as many versions of what is going on as there are people interacting in a given social space.

Classic quantitative research was supposed to be "value free" in the sense that science is supposed to be the quest for truth. Research is conducted for the sake of science, to contribute to our store of knowledge and to perpetuate a fruitful, ongoing discourse within the scientific community. Qualitative researchers, by contrast, are comfortable embracing a value-laden position. Doing so does not mean that they are biased or that they deliberately manipulate their findings in order to reach the conclusions they have approved of beforehand. Rather, it means that they are willing to acknowledge that research is conducted mainly to solve (or, at least, to ameliorate) perceived social problems—and, of course, what constitutes a "problem" can be very much in the eye of the beholder.

Quantitative research may also be used in this "applied" sense, but good quantitative studies are supposed to stand on their own as contributions to the scientific literature, whether or not they are of direct help to anyone in the "real world." By the same token, qualitative research may yield studies that are of principal interest to the scientific community; but at some level they are responses to concerns that are not always purely academic in nature. A "good" piece of quantitative research is judged by its statistical elegance and by the way it advances scientific discourse. A "good" piece of qualitative research is essentially one that can be effectively deployed for the betterment of a community. Of course, what makes something "better" is a subjective value judgment based on criteria that may include scientific judgments but that almost certainly involve politics, morality, and even aesthetics, all of which are relatively difficult to quantify and objectify.

In the last analysis, quantitative research results in a statistical analysis of trends and patterns based on relationships between or among objective data collected from a carefully chosen sample population. Qualitative research results in a descriptive, narrative account of events and behaviors. Quantitative researchers can claim that because of the nature of their sampling techniques they can project and predict outcomes in similar populations. Qualitative researchers are more typically content to provide a thorough, in-depth analysis of the single case that has been studied; that case may be thought of as illustrative of larger trends, but it is usually not possible to draw a statistically significant correlation between that case and others that might be superficially similar.

# The Eight-Step Process of Social Research

The quantitative and qualitative paradigms require researchers to equip themselves with different tools (philosophical assumptions about the nature of reality and, as we will see as we go on, specific data-collection techniques). But they both end in the same place: a concluding statement about the way things are that consumers of the research can feel confident in accepting. Moreover, both ways of doing social research involve making critical decisions at common turning points; the successful resolution of those decisions will lead to the logically effective integration of the research process, leading ultimately to that confidence-inspiring conclusion.

In this book I will discuss social research as a process consisting of eight steps. "Eight" is not a magic number; some researchers might prefer to group one or more of these steps into larger categories, thus coming up with fewer steps, while others might want to divide some of them into more minutely detailed units, thus coming up with more steps. Eight is a reasonable number to work with. The purpose of this Introduction is simply to outline the process and introduce the eight steps, each of which will then be treated in fuller detail in the chapters that follow. The eight steps of social research are:

1. **Choosing a topic** is a process guided by our understanding of issues currently important either in the academic world of the social sciences, in current events, or in personal experience.

2. **Deciding on a problem** involves settling on a specific, focused aspect of the larger topic.

3. **Conducting a literature review**—"literature" being understood as the body of published source material bearing on your general topic and the more specifically defined problem—is done to discover what is already known as well as what gaps in our knowledge currently exist.

4. **Formulating one or more research questions** guides the inquiry in the most direct fashion and therefore keeps the research from being an unfocused fishing expedition.

5. **Devising a methodological strategy** involves choosing between the quantitative or qualitative paradigms as well as selecting specific data-collection techniques that lead most efficiently to a reasonable answer to the research question(s).

6. **Collecting data** is undertaken with the basic research questions in mind, since those questions should indicate what the research is leading to. It is equally important to record the data in a form that will allow for efficient retrieval and analysis.

7. **Analyzing findings** involves looking for trends or patterns in the data and then applying social science theory to understand why those trends or patterns exist.

8. **Sharing results** allows a specific inquiry to become a part of the ongoing scientific discourse.

## SUGGESTIONS FOR FURTHER READING

In this chapter, and those that follow, the suggested readings are intended to give the beginning researcher a preliminary guide to the available resources, should he or she want to follow up on the topic or theme of the chapter. These lists should not be taken as complete bibliographies covering the entire range of literature on a given topic.

In that spirit, an excellent place to begin a detailed, comparative study of the differences between qualitative and quantitative research, and a careful analysis of the pros and cons of each pathway, is John W. Creswell (1994), *Research Design: Qualitative and Quantitative Approaches* (Thousand Oaks, CA: Sage). A comparative analysis more directly applicable to the conduct of social research is W. Lawrence Neuman (2006), *Social Research Methods: Qualitative and Quantitative Approaches*, 6th ed. (Boston: Allyn & Bacon).

A very useful outline introduction to the eight-step research process is found in James M. Henslin (2009), *Sociology, A Down-to-Earth Approach: Core Concepts*, 3rd ed. (Boston: Pearson); see in particular chapter 1.

## QUESTIONS FOR DISCUSSION

In this chapter, and those that follow, these questions can serve as a guide to your personal reflection on the topic and themes of the chapter, or they can be the basis for group discussions facilitated by your instructor.

1. Consider this research question: "Which factors lead college students to use on-campus health services?" Discuss the pros and cons of quantitative and qualitative research as ways to answer the question.

2. If you wanted to "take a survey" to answer the question about student health services, you might do so face-to-face, on the phone, through regular mail, or via e-mail. Discuss the pros and cons of each of these techniques for you as a researcher. Then discuss their pros and cons as they might appear to someone asked to participate in the survey. If the needs of you the researcher seem to be different from those of the potential respondents, which should take precedence in carrying out the project? Clearly explain and justify your reasoning.

# Chapter One

# **Choosing a Topic**

---◆◆◆---

## Social research begins with a seemingly simple, but vitally important matter: you must *select a topic*.

All of the social sciences deal with the *activities of groups of people*. This definition is sufficiently broad as to render almost any topic fair game for research. It will therefore ultimately be necessary to narrow one's focus, but I recommend beginning by casting a fairly wide net. By doing so you are likely to get an idea of the broad context into which more specific social issues can fit. It is certainly possible, for example, to select a topic based on a public policy issue currently in the news—a good indication that it is widely considered to be important. But most public policy issues turn out to be very complex, despite the fact that they are all too often reduced to bumper sticker slogans. Most important social issues have economic, political, or historical dimensions, and they touch on matters that can be deeply personal as well as matters of public concern. It is certainly possible to plan a comprehensive study that treats all of these dimensions—if one is thinking ahead to one's life work.

For a single research project, however, I prefer to begin not with an issue that already seems defined in the arena of public opinion but with an open-ended reflection on nine major social institutions. In this way you can define the problem for yourself, in your own terms—terms that make sense as the basis of research (as opposed to terms that have already become enmeshed in contentious public debate.)

The term "social institution" refers to an organized pattern of beliefs and behavior centered on basic social needs, most notably physical reproduction, cultural reproduction, the production and distribution of goods and services, the preservation of order, and the provision and maintenance of a sense of meaning and purpose. It is clear that if a society is to continue to exist, it must reproduce its membership; new members of society come about through biological means, typically within the context of the family, although they may also be incorporated through processes of immigration, which is usually regulated by laws established by governments. Once the physical survival of a society is assured in these ways, a society must then take steps to teach its body of knowledge and its values to its new members. This cultural reproduction begins with the family, but is then entrusted to educational systems of one sort or another as well as to the communications media that are used by a people. The goods and services produced by the members of a society must be distributed for the common good (in whatever way that concept may be interpreted in any given culture); hence there will be an economic system, which is dependent on the orderly, controlled actions of the community, the job once again of government, the law, and/or the military. Finally, the sense of a purpose larger than mere survival is the work of religion, often in combination with governmental and educational systems, and supported by the media.

Social scientists are not of one mind when it comes to naming the major social institutions—the organized patterns of belief and behavior that somehow act to meet basic needs. As with our list of the steps in the research process, some lists of institutions are quite long, while others result from lumping similar patterns together to create fewer headings. But a typical list—one that seems to cover those institutions that crop up in all societies, from the small-scale traditional ones to the large, complex ones—contains nine items. We can work with this list of major social institutions, which are:

1. **The family** exists primarily to regulate reproduction and to teach and protect children. It consists of networks of blood or marital relatives (kinship groups).

2. **Religion** is mainly concerned with understanding the meaning of life and the nature of right and wrong. It is composed of formal associations (congregations) of various sizes based on common beliefs, rituals, and myths and is often the vehicle for organized charity.

3. **Education** is the vehicle for the formal transmission of knowledge and skills from one generation to the next. It involves schools, both

private and public, at various levels of instruction, trained instructors, and standardized curricula.

4. **The economy** is the sum total of the means of production and the distribution of goods and services. It includes the agencies that bring owners and workers together for the purposes of production and distribution as well as the agencies (e.g., banks, stock markets) that provide for the flow of money and credit that keep the productive and distributive capacities flowing.

5. **Medicine** is concerned with both preventing illness and treating the sick. It is ultimately based on the relationship between trained healers and their patients, which may be worked out in private practices or in public or private institutional settings (clinics, hospitals) of various sizes, often conditioned by the policies of the private insurance industry and/or government insurance (e.g., the currently well-established Medicare and Medicaid programs).

6. **Politics** is the sum total of the means for allocating power, promulgating law, and preserving public order. In the United States, it is based in executive, legislative, and judicial agencies working in some sort of defined and coordinated fashion.

7. **Science** is the set of knowledge that underlies attempts to understand and master the physical (and sometimes interpersonal) environment. It is based in schools, research institutions, museums, and a network of funding support both private and public.

8. **The military** provides protection from enemies and physical support for the furtherance of national foreign policies. In the United States it includes the traditional services (army, navy, marines, air force, coast guard, national guard) as well operations like the Central Intelligence Agency and, increasingly, a network of private contractors who are paid by the government.

9. **The mass media** disseminate information and opinion. The media include television networks, radio stations, publishers, and the emerging Web-based "blogosphere."

To say that a society is defined in terms of its orderly organization is not to conclude that all societies work in perfect harmony. As we all know, societies can sometimes (often?) be shaken by conflict or other forms of persistent dysfunction. Indeed, some societies seem to thrive on discord. We will return to this point when we discuss data analysis (the work of theory in the social sciences) in chapter 7, but for the moment we can safely say that no society can long survive unless it makes some sort of concerted effort to meet the basic needs outlined above. Whether it does so in a fair and equitable manner—or whether it should even strive to do so—is another matter that we can put off to a later chapter.

It should be noted that in some traditional, small-scale, less-industrialized societies one or more of these institutions (e.g., military, mass media) may play a very small and inconspicuous role; such societies may also have informal rather than formal institutions of medicine or education. Nevertheless, the needs met by such institutions are, in fact, dealt with, even if not in the more obvious way in which they appear in the industrialized world. It should also be clear that in both industrialized and less-industrialized societies, those institutions that are operative do not work in isolation—they form a social system, influencing one another in many complex ways.

Nevertheless, for the purposes of our research agenda, it is possible to separate the social institutions so that one begins with a fairly well-bounded institutional context into which more specifically defined social problems may fall. There is certainly a link between, for example, the role of the mass media in disseminating information and the activities of politicians in formulating public policy, but a study grounded in an analysis of the role of the mass media will be significantly different in emphasis from one grounded in research into the mechanics of the legislative process itself. It will therefore be helpful for you to begin with an institutional context that in general is of most interest to you; you can then define a more narrowly focused theme as it is related to that general context.

## The Sample Project: Selecting a Topic

The project that will be my example throughout this book begins with my long-standing research and teaching interest in two of the nine social institutions: medicine and religion. In pre-industrial societies, these two were almost always linked, as religious specialists such as shamans were usually also the primary healers within the community. In modern societies, by contrast, there is a long history of separating the two—we tend to think of medicine as a scientific endeavor, grounded in empirical, experimental, and/or naturalistic "reason," while we define religion as the realm of faith, the mystical, and the supernatural. But as noted above, religion is also concerned with giving a community a sense of right and wrong; moreover, as an impetus to "charity," it often stands behind our collective impulse to help others and to promote the welfare of the entire group rather than just look out for ourselves. My own interests have therefore been at this particular intersection of religion and medicine—not "faith healing" or the use of non-Western healing techniques as "alternative medicine" in our own society, but in the ways in which organized medicine in a modern society is an expression of moral and ethical precepts derived from our historical faith traditions. As you can see, I have phrased this connection with medicine/health care as the primary institutional focus, with religion as the underlying source of our widespread collective decision to make health care a public concern.

The World Health Organization (WHO) defines "health" as a state of complete physical, mental, and social well-being, and not merely the absence of disease and infirmity. This definition clearly shifts the practice of medicine away from the strictly biological realm and into the domains of society and culture. All humans live in organized, ongoing communities of one sort or another, and the values, behavioral norms, and expectations of those communities shape our ideas about health and also influence the degree to which we have access to health care and the ways in which we are exposed to risks to our health.

Our health is certainly a matter of how we feel, but it is a lot more besides. We must always factor in what the people around us think—their perception of how we are doing is a major influence on how we feel. An individual may feel fine, but if significant others in his or her community keep saying things like, "You don't seem like yourself," or "Is there something wrong?" that person may feel impelled to go to the doctor to get checked out. The doctor, in turn, may perform various tests that indicate that there is, indeed, something wrong even if the person is as yet experiencing no overt symptoms. Once the doctor has confirmed one's friends' evaluation that something is wrong, the person is very likely to start feeling a lot less perky.

Social scientists have long understood that illness, in addition to compromising a person's biological and/or psychological well-being, is also a threat to the social order. A "sick" person is apt to miss work or school or any of the innumerable other functional responsibilities that people have in society. There is probably no one reading this book who has not at one time or another wondered, "Am I sick enough to stay home?" and thus risk inconveniencing others. On the other hand, there are certainly some people who rather enthusiastically embrace the "sick role" as a way of getting out of an unpleasant obligation and/or of getting sympathy. In any case, we can surely understand why the WHO defines health as more than the absence of disease, which is a purely biomedical condition.

Being "ill" implies that whether or not one has a definable disease, one feels at less than an optimal level of well-being and, moreover, is treated (either with annoyance or compassionate concern as the case may be) by others as being un-well.

In our society, we have designated an entire class of health care professionals as the ones empowered to officially declare people healthy or ill and hence to validate their adoption of the "sick role." The opinions of our friends and family may be among the primary motives that lead us into the hands of the professionals, but it is the latter who give us sanctioned permission to access all the resources that our modern society can mobilize to overcome illness and promote health. For example, as an instructor I am often confronted by students who are in obviously bad shape, but, like every other instructor in the world, I always insist that students have a "doctor's note" in order for me to excuse their absence, let them postpone handing in an assignment, or take a makeup exam, as the case may be. The evidence of my own eyes, that a student is crawling on all fours and has entered the building with vultures circling overhead, is not good enough—without the "doctor's note," no student (or worker in a place of business or an athlete on the field of competition, for that matter) is officially "sick" and thus excused from regular activities and responsibilities.

Doctors, nurses, pharmacists, and a host of other professional and paraprofessional caregivers are in effect the *gatekeepers* to the health care system. Gatekeeping of this sort would have been unnecessary in premodern societies, in which the family circle of someone thought to be ailing could directly contact the medicine man/woman, who would come to the home and do whatever was considered appropriate. In many cases, the medicine man/woman would be part of the local community or family circle and would know about the problem without having to be specifically notified. But as societies became larger and more heterogeneous, and as medical practice became a privileged body of expertise that could be exercised only by those who have extensive and exclusive training, there have come to be many more steps between the "sick" person and his or her treatment. Hence, we speak of a health care *system* rather than of "health care" plain and simple. Indeed, so great is the power and prestige we have given to medical professionals as a result of their specialized and monopolistic knowledge that some social scientists have made the claim that health care professionals occupy the same role in our society that shamans and other ritual leaders of community prayer and sacrifice did in more traditional societies—another interesting, if metaphorical, crossover between medicine and religion.

Another trend much commented upon by social scientists is the "medicalization of society." Any number of behaviors that were once considered merely odd or annoying have been given medical labels and are treated as medical problems by certified health care professionals. The child who was once "naughty" now has Attention Deficit Disorder. The socially awkward person is now liable to be diagnosed as suffering from Asperger's Syndrome. The "picky eater" of old may now have a serious "eating disorder." Conditions that were once considered manifestations of the supernatural (e.g., trances and hallucinations) are now likely to be thought of as symptoms of a medical condition (e.g., epilepsy) or a psychological disturbance (e.g., schizophrenia). Behaviors that were once thought of as symptoms of moral turpitude may now be medicalized into treatable syndromes (e.g., sex or gambling addiction, alcoholism, drug dependency).

The medicalization of society means that people who exhibit characteristics that society as a whole finds remarkable in a negative way are apt to be dealt with, not by the criminal justice system (although many of them may end up there), but by the medical system. Doctors and the medicines they alone are empowered to prescribe have become important mediators for the control of unacceptable behavior. Those who do not respond to treatment end up in hospitals or other kinds of medically based institutions, where they are segregated from society. It is certainly true that people can be said to be hospitalized or institutionalized "for their own good." But it is no less true that people are hospitalized or institutionalized because their family and friends have given up hope of personally helping them.

Doctors and their professional associates have always had the lives of patients in their hands; in effect, any kind of medical treatment is to some degree a matter of life or death. But as a result of the medicalization of society, doctors and their professional associates have also become the arbiters of public policy relating to health care. Several decades ago there was a great public outcry over the campaign to fluoridate public drinking water. There were many who feared that the government was illegitimately tampering with our "precious bodily fluids" and who saw a nefarious communist plot against the purity of this most vital of all resources. But once the medical community presented its scientific arguments in favor of fluoridation, opposition was gradually pushed to the sidelines as the easily caricatured obsession of fringe-group nuts.

As of this writing, there is some vocal opposition to the mandating of vaccines against the H1N1 ("swine flu") virus; some people simply object to being told what to do, while others have a seemingly more rational reluctance to line up for an "untested" vaccine against a disease that, while very widespread, is not (yet) a scary mass killer. But since the medical community seems united in explicating the risks to the general public of allowing too many people to opt out of the vaccination, the opposition can be readily dismissed as misguided or irrational.

There are those who see a major exception to this pattern: health insurance companies often seem to override the judgment of doctors when it comes to deciding which treatments will be compensated— which, in turn, tends to determine which treatments are offered to patients. It is certainly true that doctors and insurers often have different standards for evaluating the necessity of treatment: doctors are concerned with what will be most effective for the patient under their direct care, while insurance companies are mainly concerned with the profits they can return to their stockholders. These demands seem to be incompatible, and the apparent ascendancy of the insurance point of view suggests that doctors aren't as powerful and prestigious as they have been made out to be. But that conclusion does not take into account that both doctors and insurance companies are part of the same system—in a society like ours, one could not function without the other. Whether grudgingly or not, they ultimately are parts of the same dynamic that defines the ways in which illness in our society is diagnosed and people receive health care.

The evolution of the modern health care system is a process into which we can contextualize many of the trends of modern society—the specialization of knowledge and the extreme division of labor in our economic system; the apparent predominance of market forces over strictly humanitarian concerns; the removal of health care (and education, for that matter) from the family circle to impersonal institutions. For all these reasons, I chose to begin my project with a focus on the social institution of medicine, which is thus the *topic* of my research. Please note that having phrased my interest in medicine in terms of humanitarian issues dealing with the morality of health care (as seen in contradistinction to the exigencies of "social control") I have set myself on a path of qualitative research. I could certainly have chosen a different way to deal with modern medicine, for example by studying the impact of "medicalizing" various behavior patterns on workplace productivity. Doing so might logically lead to a quantitative study of labor market trends and economic indicators. Both kinds of study are, I believe, important and relevant. But having begun with a particular kind of topical statement, further decision points represented by later steps in the process seem to be clearly foreshadowed.

## SUGGESTIONS FOR FURTHER READING

A widely cited early exposition of the concept of social institutions and basic needs is found in David E. Aberle, A. K. Cohen, A. K. Davis, M. J. Leng, and F. N. Sutton (1950), "The Functional Prerequisites of a Society," *Ethics* 60:100–111. The concept was elaborated in a manner still accepted by most sociologists by Raymond W. Mack and Calvin P. Bradford (1979), *Transforming America: Patterns of Social Change* (New York: Random House).

Hugh R. Leavell and E. Gurney Clark (1965), *Preventive Medicine for the Doctor in His Community: An Epidemiologic Approach, 3rd ed.* (New York: McGraw-Hill) includes an excellent, early analysis of the modern, WHO-inspired view of health and illness. Eliot Freidson (1970), *Profession of Medicine* (New York: Dodd, Mead) was a pioneer in the analysis of the role of the doctor in modern society as analogous to that of the shaman/healer of traditional society. The sociologist Talcott Parsons popularized the concept of the "sick role," a concept he dealt with in several articles over the years. His original work on that theme, however, is found in his classic 1951 book *The Social System* (New York: Free Press).

Irving K. Zola was one of the most influential scholars in the field of the "medicalization of society." In addition to his research efforts, he was a tireless advocate for the rights of the "disabled." He came to understand that the conditions we call "disabilities" are more often than not simply variations from the social norm; the application of the label, however, turns them into stigmatized medical conditions. A man who was "slow" back in the days when America was mainly a rural society in need of strong manual laborers could find a useful role in society; now, he would be sent to special schools or perhaps even institutionalized, as our information-based society no longer has a place for those with "strong backs, weak minds." Two important works by Zola are his 1972 article, "Medicine as an Institution of Social Control," *Sociological Review* 20:487–504; and his 1983 book, *Socio-Medical Inquiries* (Philadelphia: Temple University Press).

The most widely cited history of modern medicine, and the most detailed chronicle of its transformation into an institution of specialized, monopolistic knowledge, power, and prestige is Paul Starr (1982), *The Social Transformation of American Medicine* (New York: Basic Books).

## QUESTIONS FOR DISCUSSION

1. Select any one of the nine social institutions that you think could be the topical context for a piece of research that you conduct yourself. Write a brief essay on some of the major trends and patterns that social scientists have identified as important in this institution in the modern world. (If you select "medicine," you may either elaborate on the several trends I have introduced in this chapter, or you may think of other aspects of the social institution of medicine that seem more pertinent to you.)

2. Discuss my choice of a topic. Granted the overlap between medicine and religion, what difference, if any, would it make if I contextualized my interest mainly within the institution of religion rather than mainly in medicine?

# Chapter Two

# **Deciding on a Problem**

———◆◆◆———

You are now at a point at which
you can *define a problem*
within your larger topical area.

It is clearly impossible to conduct a research project on something as vast as "the social institution of medicine." One must therefore discern some more narrowly defined aspect of such an institution that seems to be problematic—that is, in need of some sort of clarification.

For a social scientist, something may be defined as a "social problem" because it represents an area in which very little research has been conducted. We can also define a "social problem" as something more specific: a condition or a pattern of behavior that harms some segment(s) of a society to the extent that there is a consensus that "something needs to be done" to improve that condition or ameliorate that pattern of behavior. The first definition would lead us to "basic research" in which our primary concern is to contribute to the discourse of science. The second definition would lead us to an "applied" form of research, since addressing a social problem with this mind-set is designed to bring about some sort of action that will bring about change in the society; our findings will generate interest among people beyond those who read scientific journals.

A number of important problems encompassed by the institution of medicine may not, at first glance, appear to be "social" in nature at all. For example, an epidemic infectious disease becomes a problem because large populations do not have sufficient immunity to the pathogen—a biomedical issue. One could not hope to address such a problem (e.g., the global spread of HIV/AIDS) without first understanding the nature of the virus, its means of spreading through a population, its effects on the human body, and the ways to treat it once it occurs. But it is equally clear that a problem like an epidemic disease also has a social component. The transmission of HIV/AIDS is directly linked to human behavior with regard to sex and other activities (both licit and illicit) that involve the exchange of bodily fluids—behaviors that are strongly influenced by cultural and community norms, values, and expectations. No study of the HIV/AIDS epidemic would be complete without adding the social/cultural dimension to the biomedical one.

To be sure, a "problem" mainly exists in the eye of the beholder. For example, many people still think that HIV/AIDS is problem segmented to homosexuals, the sexually promiscuous, intravenous drug users, and people in the Third World. As another example, economically well-to-do members of Congress who enjoy generous government-sponsored health care cannot see why there are people who think our health insurance system is in need of reform. Liberal-minded middle-class people who are not personally racist or sexist or homophobic might think these matters were problematic in less enlightened days gone by and may wonder why some groups continue to complain about them. In sum, we tend not to see a problem until it hits home. Social scientists therefore cannot rely simply on their personal experience to tell them what is or is not a problem worthy of research. Thus, they have developed a kind of checklist to help them determine if an issue is truly a "social problem" in the way we have defined it. They will ask the following:

- Is there a public outcry about this condition or behavior that goes beyond an obvious group concerned only with its own self-interest? Is there sentiment demanding that "something must be done"?

- Does the condition or behavior reflect some sort of discrepancy between social ideals and social reality? (For example, in our society, we believe that everyone is equal before the law. What, then, of laws that deny some groups the right to do something that is perfectly legal for everyone else as was the case with voting among African Americans in the pre-Civil Rights era, or with marriage among same-sex couples today?)

- Is there some reasonable way to address the problem? (For example, some people are very concerned about "global warming," but in the face of the enormous and apparently endless complexity of the factors involved in that condition, they may throw up their hands in despair, perhaps believing that the steps they take to reduce their own "carbon footprint" will be a meaningless drop in the bucket.)

We can use analogous criteria to evaluate whether a scientific (as opposed to a social) issue is worthy of research. We might, for example, ask (1) whether an issue is one that a broad spectrum of scientific opinion has agreed is in need of further discussion, (2) whether there is a discrepancy between what is empirically known about a proposed topic and what our dominant theories have taught us to expect, and (3) whether the issue is amenable to study by valid, reliable research methods. (Lots of people wonder if God exists, but the answer to that question resides in the realm of faith, not science.)

It should be pointed out that an issue, be it scientific or social, should not be rejected as an object of study just because it does not meet all of those criteria. My personal view is that only the third criterion (whether it can, in fact, be studied using recognized techniques of scientific research) is vital. If you have a burning desire to study something that is of concern only to a seemingly unimportant fringe minority, you should feel free to go ahead with your research—the worst that can happen is that you will be ignored, although it is entirely possible that you will end up illuminating the seemingly trivial matter in such a way that provokes a major shift in public opinion. If you can establish the relevance of your research, then no problem is too small to be considered. Moreover, conducting research on an issue that you are really interested in will almost certainly make the research stronger than if you are doing a project just because "they" think it is important.[1]

Critics of academe delight in pointing to apparently ridiculous research projects that win financial support and are published in the journals. For example, a recent story in the news concerned the article, "Are Full or Empty Beer Bottles Sturdier to Break the Human Skull?" It appeared in the presumably prestigious *Journal of Forensic and Legal Medicine,* although it was widely lampooned as a prime example of money- and time-wasting pseudo-research. But as it turns out, the researchers had the last laugh. In Switzerland, there was a vigorous public debate about the advisability of banning beer bottles in "situations which involve risk of human conflicts." The research concluded that empty or full, a beer bottle is sturdy enough to break a skull before the skull breaks the bottle. Public policy in Switzerland was duly swayed. And so, while hardly earth-shaking, this presumably silly piece of research proved to be very useful in at least one part of the world.

# The Sample Project: Defining a Problem

The sample research project, described in chapter 1, began with the decision to focus on the institution of medicine in U.S. society. A further decision, to look at the moral/ethical dimension of health care (as distinct from, say, the clinical, biological, or epidemiological aspects of medicine in the modern world), led to conducting a qualitative, rather than a quantitative, study. Once a specific research problem has been chosen, you should consider whether the research should be "basic" or "applied" in nature.

In the case of my own project, several predisposing factors led me to the applied approach. Most of my career has been spent conducting applied research; I have often done research while in the role of consultant to one or another community-based or government agency dealing with a particular issue—in my case mostly in the field of mental health. Moreover, I have been a faculty member in a department that has for more than three decades taken applied social science as its core mission, particularly in terms of the training of graduate students and in the research and service activities expected of its faculty. I certainly value the contributions of basic research to our understanding of health care issues; indeed, we would have little to apply without having a body of empirical data and a fund of theoretical/analytical perspectives to begin with. But my own personal and departmental inclinations made the choice of applied research for this project an easy one.

It happened that in the months prior to beginning this new project I had been asked to join a board of community advisors at a large teaching hospital that has institutional links to the colleges of medicine and nursing at my university. Thus, immersed in issues pertinent to the work of an urban hospital, I decided that my study of the moral/ethical dimension of health care should be based in the hospital. It is obvious that the health care system in a complex society such as that in the U.S. involves many component parts—private practitioners, research institutions, insurance companies, to name just a few, in addition to hospitals of various sizes and various types. Any one of them would be a reasonable locus for research. A particular hospital was, however, a logical focus for me because I was already involved in that setting.

There are, to be sure, many hospitals in the United States, and one could certainly do an interesting quantitative study comparing data that have been collected and that are publicly available about any number of aspects of the work of those hospitals. My commitment to qualitative research, however, suggested that instead of trying to discern trends or patterns that were statistically valid in generic ways in "the contemporary American hospital," I would conduct an in-depth case study of one hospital. The research method of the ethnographic case study will be discussed in greater detail in the chapter on research methods, but suffice it to say at this point that such a method yields an intensive descriptive analysis that can be shown to be illustrative of the whole, although it cannot (and should never claim to be able to) establish statistically valid general trends.

It would be interesting to conduct an ethnographic case study that would treat a particular hospital as if it were a tribe or village that might be studied by cultural anthropologists or as an ethnic neighborhood that might be studied by sociologists. Doing so would yield a purely descriptive study that could add to our knowledge base about how hospitals actually work (i.e., getting at the everyday activities, informal structures, and interactions that go beyond the formal organizational flowcharts to demonstrate how the place really goes about its business). Such a study would probably fall under the heading of "basic research." But for applied research, it would be necessary to refine the problem statement so that the research could result in an analysis that would involve making concrete recommendations for improving an aspect of the hospital's work that is perceived to be in need of amelioration.

I was therefore very interested when discussions at community board meetings turned to a matter that seemed to fit especially well with my own developing research interests. The hospital was very concerned with nurturing a more "caring" approach and with promoting an image of itself as a center of care to the community at large. It might seem odd to think that this is an issue at all—after all, we commonly speak of hospitals as part of a system of health *care,* and we assume that patients in a hospital are being cared for in an appropriate manner. But we also know that most people think of hospitals with dread, not only because they are places of sickness and death but because even if someone is in fact being healed, the context in which the healing takes place is anything but comforting. Hospitals are notorious for their impersonality and for their emphasis on the technology of treatment often at the expense of compassion. The image of being "hooked up to machines" springs to mind far more often than that of having one's fevered brow soothed by a compassionate caregiver. The hospital board on which I served was trying to convince the hospital's (to which I will give the pseudonym City General Hospital, or CGH) administrators to adopt an "ethic of care" as its guiding principle. The administrators pointed out that a number of steps had already been taken in that direction, but they were not sure about ways to enhance that approach.

I therefore began to formulate an idea of a workable research problem: to conduct an in-depth case study of CGH's existing "ethic of care" measures and to make some feasible (i.e., not pie-in-the-sky) recommendations for implementing both ethical and caring practices. I suggested this plan at a meeting of the board, and it was agreed that I should proceed to develop a proposal that could be taken to the hospital administrators.

It should be noted that applied projects often arise in the minds of the agency itself; the bureaucrats have already identified both a topic and a problem. In other cases, funding sources may publish "requests for proposals" (RFPs), soliciting researchers to submit fleshed-out project proposals that respond to the agency's original idea. RFPs may result in either applied or basic research, depending on the needs and policies of the funding source. In any case, the researcher's first task when responding to an RFP is to tweak the bureaucrats' idea into something that is workable in terms of social science research. But I have chosen this particular example precisely because the idea was mine to begin with; I can thus illustrate all eight steps of the research process in terms of how one researcher developed a project.

## SUGGESTIONS FOR FURTHER READING

"Social problems" is a field of study within sociology with an identity all its own. The number of works in this tradition is enormous, but you may want to ground your reading of this chapter with a simple, basic textbook. One that is readily available is by Diana Kendall (2007), *Social Problems in a Diverse Society, 4th ed.* (Boston: Allyn & Bacon).

Connoisseurs of absurdity might be interested in the *Annals of Improbable Research*, a "science-humor magazine" that highlights "achievements that first make people laugh, and then make them think." It is an amusing rebuke to those who disdain research that seems to deal with unimportant matters; such research can, in fact, end up making a valid contribution to science or public policy, or both. In any case, the beer bottle study discussed in this chapter was awarded the 2009 Annual Ig-Nobel Peace Prize (Ig-Nobel prizes are a parody of the real Nobel prizes) by the *Annals* staff because of its contribution to keeping the peace in Swiss drinking establishments. The judges were all winners of genuine Nobel Prizes in various fields of science.

Hospital ethnography as a field of social scientific study is surveyed in a series of articles edited by S. van der Geest and Kaja Finkler (2004) in vol. 59 of the journal *Social Science and Medicine*.

---

## QUESTIONS FOR DISCUSSION

1. With your selected social institution in mind as a general topic, focus on a researchable problem within that topic.

   a. Decide whether you want to do a piece of basic or applied research. Explain why. State the problem in a way that clearly demonstrates how and why your project would fall within that category.

   b. Discuss the ways you have come to understand that this problem is a worthwhile focus for research: personal experience? current events? something you have studied in another class?

2. Discuss my choice of a research problem. To what extent does it meet the criteria of a "social problem" as outlined in this chapter? In what ways does it not fit? Does the lack of fit automatically relegate the project to the "improbable research" category with the Swiss beer bottles? If so, why? If not, why not?

3. Other than the fact that I was already affiliated with a specific hospital that was somewhat interested in my research, what factors recommend a hospital as the focus of a case study in social aspects of modern medicine?

---

## NOTE

[1] But a word of caution: it may be wise to avoid doing research on an issue that is of intense emotional and personal importance to you, as it will be very difficult for you to remain unbiased. The issue should engage your scientific interest as well as your social conscience, but not to the point where you become an unreasonable partisan. Only you, however, can decide in the last analysis whether you are "too close" to an issue to do a credible job as a social scientist.

# Chapter Three

# Conducting a Literature Review

The third step is
to *review the literature*
pertinent to your problem.

When researchers refer to "the literature" they mean the body of published sources that contribute information and analytical insight to a given issue or topic. A literature review is a critical account of that published material. (Please note that in scholarly language, "critical" does not necessarily mean negative; criticism simply means a reasoned evaluation, whether it is positive, negative, or neutral.) In traditional research, "the literature" usually meant books published by reputable presses and/ or peer-reviewed articles in scholarly journals. The definition also included papers read at scholarly conferences. In traditional scholarship, a literature review was looking at a stand-alone publication of an annotated bibliography (such as the comments in my "Suggestions for Further Reading" sections, but far more extensive). For our purposes, however, a literature review is part of a larger process of research.

A literature review is the one aspect of good scientific (including social scientific) research that is common to all types of research. While there are variations in problem definition or (as we shall see in later chapters) in methodologies, theories, and presentation strategies, a literature review follows a standard process (although of course, the content of the literature will vary) whether the research is basic or applied, quantitative or qualitative. One important exception to this generalization, however, concerns applied research, which may rely on a body of literature that is found in reports submitted to sponsoring agencies and is not published in standard scholarly sources. Reports submitted to public agencies are usually available to other researchers.[1] On the other hand, reports submitted to private funding sources may be considered the property of the agency itself and may be available only if the researcher is affiliated with the same agency.

"The literature" as a whole consists of two main elements: (1) *primary sources,* which are those based on research done by the author him- or herself, and (2) *secondary sources,* which are summaries of others' research such as those found in textbooks or encyclopedias. Although scholars hold primary sources as the gold standard of research, do not neglect the secondary sources, which may well provide a concise introduction to a topic that a newcomer to the field will find more useful than an immediate plunge into the more specialized, technical primary literature. Moreover, secondary sources often include bibliographies (i.e., lists of references) of classic or important works on the topic. Some scholars dismiss secondary literature because it is "not cutting edge"; that is, it represents the established view rather than the newest, most innovative information and analysis. But you will eventually get to the latter, and there is certainly nothing wrong with allowing yourself to get the lay of the land, which is an overview that secondary sources are very well suited to providing.

Modern scholars have broadened their concept of "the literature" to include photo archives, films/videos, audio recordings, and museum exhibits. The most important new addition to "the literature" is material found on the Internet, a source that challenges ancient notions of just what it means to be "published." Material on the Internet is often not edited or even reviewed—anyone can post a blog about any old thing and even an online encyclopedia like Wikipedia is largely unfiltered and cannot always be taken at face value (although its creators are beginning to take steps to better ensure its accuracy). The newer media often lack the obvious markers of legitimate scholarly status, but they can certainly open up a wealth of resources, as long as they are used with care and discretion. Be sure that any Web site that you want to use has an identified author or is sponsored by a group or agency that you have reason to trust. Try to use sites that are designed for use by educated audiences; it is fine to begin with sites clearly marked "for dummies" as long as they do not constitute the sum total of your research base. Make sure that the site is updated frequently. Try, if at all possible, to verify the information on one site by comparing it to one or more other sites dealing with the same material.

In olden times (when your humble author was a graduate student) all literature reviews began (and ended) with the library card catalogue, a quaint device that no longer exists, and that most students have probably never even seen. The card catalogue contained an index card for each book in a particular library's collection, cross-referenced by author, title, and subject. There were also massive print volumes of the *Reader's Guide to Periodical Literature*, which listed every article published in most of the prominent journals. For books or back copies of journals that the library did not have in its possession, there was interlibrary loan service, which required you, the researcher, to search through (printed) copies of the card catalogues of other libraries; when the desired book was found, your own library staff would arrange to have that book sent for your limited-time use. Journal articles could be copied (I was fortunate enough to have gone to school at the dawn of the Xerox Age) and sent as well. It was a tedious, time-consuming process (and furthermore, we had to walk to the library in the snow, uphill in both directions).

Nowadays, of course, we have the luxury of using the Internet to locate the materials we need, whether they are in print or (increasingly) in electronic form. There are, however, a few pitfalls that the researcher must try to avoid lest he or she lapse into an uncritical dependence on Google or some other search engine. Internet search engines work best when we conduct a search using very specific terms—indeed the very nature of most of them requires us to be very precise. Doing so, however, has the disadvantage of pulling up only those items that seem to be most closely related to the specific search terms, at least in the minds of those who compose the algorithms that yield search results. This outcome may be fine if one is simply looking for information. It is not so good if one is looking for ways to understand that information. For example, much of my research in recent decades has dealt with adults with mental retardation; however, my greatest inspiration for ways to understand the situation of such people as they negotiate their lives in the community beyond the state institution came from an author who was primarily concerned with the behavior of alcoholics. The two conditions are certainly not related, but there are definite commonalities in the ways in which people with stigmatized medical conditions try to manage the impressions they make on society at large. I would probably have missed these insights had I limited myself to reading only studies written specifically about people with mental retardation.

Rather than randomly "Googling" your topic/problem, you will find it more efficient to use existing databases. A database is a collection of data that has been selected, organized, and made available for searching—it saves you from having to pull together all the scattered bits of information that can be gleaned from your Google search. Any database consists of data (which can be text, numbers, or pictures) organized into records made up of searchable fields. Many of the databases that will be of use to students are produced by government agencies, libraries, and scholarly associations, and they are usually free for you to use as an individual; the reference librarian at your campus library will help you identify and use the ones that seem most likely to give you the kind of information you need. But there are other databases that charge a fee; you will either have to pay to use them, or visit a library that has paid for a subscription and allows users to access them. Full-text databases contain the entire article that you are looking for; it can be downloaded and printed.

Reviewing the literature in this broad sense, of course, can be a nearly endless process—indeed it must seem so to doctoral students writing formal dissertations. But a thorough, touch-all-possible-bases literature review is neither possible nor even desirable when the matter at hand is a small-scale research project. The bottom line is that the literature review should be sufficient to give you a good idea of what is known about a given topic so that you do not end up wasting your time reinventing the wheel. Equally important, a sufficient literature review should give you a good idea about what gaps might exist—what *don't* we know about this problem, and is it feasible to fill in those gaps?

## The Sample Project: Reviewing the Literature

My sample project began with a general interest in the social institution of medicine in the contemporary United States, with an emphasis on the moral/ethical dimension of health care. As a result of participation on a community advisory board, I identified the hospital as the component of health that I wanted to study in depth. Current discussion by the board led me to identify the emergence of an "ethic of caring" as a problematic aspect of the work of the modern hospital. As a qualitative researcher I was inclined to conduct an ethnographic case study of a particular hospital rather than a survey of hospitals in general. As an applied social scientist I wanted to study how that hospital understood and carried out plans to achieve an "ethic of caring" so as to come up with some feasible recommendations for improving the system.

The next step was to review the literature. Several classic works in both cultural anthropology and sociology proved to be invaluable, as did the contemporary literature on biomedical ethics. The somewhat controversial literature on "corporate culture" was also very helpful, although it had to be used with some caution as social scientists continue to be suspicious about this extension of the concept of "culture" and as the notion of corporate culture itself goes in and out of fashion with corporate managers with some degree of frequency. A great deal has been written about the ethic of caring in journals designed specifically for hospital administrators. CGH, I discovered, had also produced an impressive collection of internal reports, directives, committee minutes, and memoranda dealing with the topic, and they were available to me as a member of the board. The results of my literature review can be summarized as follows:

Social scientists have long emphasized the degree to which modern hospitals are products of a "cult of efficiency." In some ways, this designation has positive connotations; who, after all, would want to be treated in a hospital that wasn't efficient? But for the most part the term is used in a negative sense: hospitals are believed to value technical expertise and assembly-line processing of patients above all else. Numerous studies in both the scholarly and popular genres have characterized hospitals as depersonalizing institutions in which patients are reduced to numbers on charts. They are stripped of their dignity and individuality on the assumption that doing so will make for maximally efficient operations.

Hospitals, however, are not unfeeling monoliths. If only to court public opinion in the communities they serve, they strive in various ways to promote themselves as "caring" institutions. It is generally understood that "care" will always be subordinated to "efficiency" when the bottom line is calculated, but there have been apparently sincere attempts at modifying traditional attitudes. Harvard's medical school, for example, is training doctors for "empathy" by pairing them up with individual patients whom they follow over the course of many months in the health care system. The Robert Wood Johnson Foundation has for the past several years been sending copies of a book on humanistic perspectives on medicine to all students newly admitted to any medical school in the United States.

One attempt at structural change involves the inclusion of pastoral care (i.e., the chaplaincy or religious ministry services) in multidisciplinary care teams. Chaplains have always been part of the hospital scene, but they were more often than not clergy from the community who came in only to visit members of their own congregations. Staff chaplains, by contrast, define the hospital itself as their primary ministry site; they are specially trained and certified to attend to spiritual and religious concerns and to offer comfort and support to patients, families of patients, staff, and physicians. They come from a variety of faith traditions but are available to patients and staff of all faiths (or of no faith in particular) on a regular basis. The goal of a pastoral care department is to offer care that is appropriate, ecumenical, accessible, and integrated with the care offered by other members of the health care team. Chaplaincy training is now coordinated by the Association for Clinical Pastoral Education (ACPE), which vigorously promotes an enhanced role for hospital chaplains. Unlike the in-and-out, prayer-saying, hand-holding community clergy, certified hospital chaplains are encouraged to take on a variety of roles in full partnership with doctors, nurses, and social workers. As a result, pastoral care departments are often at the center of a hospital's efforts to show that it cares, even as it keeps up the highest standards of efficiency and technical expertise.

A second front in the establishment of an ethic of caring is the hospital ethics committee (HEC). The Joint Commission on Accreditation of Healthcare Organizations (JCAHO) mandates that all organizations seeking accreditation have a "mechanism for the consideration of ethical issues arising in the care of patients." Such a "mechanism" must also "provide education to caregivers *and* patients on ethical issues." Over the past 25 years, the HEC has emerged as the "mechanism" of choice. It is clear from national comparative studies that HECs have decisively changed the landscape of hospital operations—although the quality of that impact remains as open to question as it was when HECs were introduced.

HECs are significantly different from both ethics review boards at primarily research-oriented institutions and high-level policy boards. The HEC is *case specific*; while it may certainly draw upon ethical principles of a general nature articulated in other settings, its primary function is to respond in "real time" to highly particularized problems in need of immediate redress. Moreover, the HEC has an explicitly educational function; not only is it reactive when a specific case comes up, but it is also supposed to be proactive in informing key players about the ethical ramifications of situations in which they commonly find themselves.

The JCAHO expects that a consultation on a pending issue or a review of a case already completed can be requested by any member of the medical staff, or by other health care professionals working in affiliation with the hospital, patient, or family member. It should be noted that most hospitals now also provide a "patient advocate" attached to each treatment unit; it is typically such a professional (usually either a nurse or social worker by training) who brings a patient's concerns before the committee. The advocate, however, is generally permitted only to present the case; he or she does not participate in committee deliberations. In most cases, the committee acts as a body to investigate, discuss, and reach a decision. It is, however, becoming more common to delegate some of these functions to smaller consultation teams or subcommittees, or even to an outside ethics consultant working as a committee of one. The latter solution may be preferred at very large institutions with a great many cases to consider, but in such cases it is a solution of expediency rather than of conscious philosophy. Nevertheless, there is a tacit assumption that both subcommittees and "committees of the whole" have moral authority only to the degree to which consensus is achieved. By contrast, the solitary outside expert is authoritative only to the extent that his or her credentials and expertise are widely recognized.

The concept of a *corporate* ethics panel supplementing (or even superseding) individual hospital committees when the hospitals are part of larger corporate systems is just beginning to find acceptance. Corporate officers, who are—more often than not—businesspeople rather than health care professionals, tend to draw a clear distinction between what happens to patients and what happens in the finance or human resources offices, focusing more on making a profit and keeping employees happy than on making sure the wide-ranging needs of patient care are met. The long-term untenability of this management strategy (which is referred to as the "silo effect" because it segregates several administrative operations in separate departments as if they were different kinds of grain in their distinct silos) is an emerging theme in the literature on corporate culture in the hospital setting.

It is clear that members of HECs must be conversant with the field of , but their approach is specifically applied and case driven rather than concerned with the articulation of general philosophical principles. They may deal with policy formation, but only with regard to the mission and operating procedures of their own institutions; they do not intend to establish precedents to be followed elsewhere. HECs have, in fact, tended to shy away from making decisions that appear to break new philosophical ground; they often act as if they would prefer to use some authoritative yet accessible manual (a sort of *Bioethics for Dummies,* perhaps) that spells everything out for them. For example, much is made of the four cardinal virtues of bioethics: autonomy, beneficence, justice, and non-maleficence. An ethically sound decision is said to respond to these values.

In the case of a patient deciding to forgo life-sustaining treatment, the claims of patient autonomy (the right to choose) have certainly been paramount. But they could be seen to be enhanced by the claims of beneficence (since the decision would serve the patient's best interests as he or she sees them) and justice (since the same right could be extended to all, without prejudice). It would also skirt the question of non-maleficence, since it does not involve a physician actively withholding or misapplying treatment against the patient's wishes. Other common issues, however, are not so neatly folded into the guidebook's categories. Questions about the treatment of seriously ill newborns, appropriate use of new reproductive technologies, conflicts between health care teams and family surrogates, HIV testing for health care professionals, and decisions about futile treatment are among those about which no clear philosophical consensus has been achieved.

Following an established rule book (the *deontological* approach of classical ethics) does not automatically lead to consensus. But performing some sort of moral cost/benefit calculation (the *consequentialist* approach of classical ethics) has proven to be equally unsatisfactory. After all, physicians may arguably predict the immediate organic outcomes of a medical decision, but it is decidedly another matter for them to predict long-term psychosocial consequences for the patient and his or her family and friends. Since the classic ethical theories are inadequate, there have been calls to adopt other perspectives, such as feminist ethics, the ethics of caring, clinical ethics, narrative ethics, casuistry, and virtue ethics. Whatever advantages such systems may have in the marketplace of ideas, they are not notably better than the older theories in solving the basic issues of HECs. Both classical and contemporary ethics perspectives are useful for establishing very broad principles; nevertheless, an HEC must deal with the fact that very specific ethical decisions based on those principles can land the institution in the midst of costly litigation. It is no wonder that more often than not HECs favor positions that are narrowly *legal* rather than ones that are *moral* in a more general sense.

Despite this apparent philosophical impasse, the supporters of HECs often express the hope that *when the committee is doing its job well* (a big leap of faith in some cases), it should not perform as a group of "ethics experts," as if it were a panel drawn from the faculty of a prestigious university's philosophy department. Rather, it should function as a community that allows for the safe (i.e., confidential) discussion of issues concerning human dignity and respect; it should also facilitate, rather than impede, the making of patient care decisions that serve as solutions to knotty problems of an immediate, case-based nature. In short, it *might* become a vehicle, within the hospital's organizational and structural operations, for a meaningful paradigm shift at the level of corporate culture.

Prior to the 1980s, hospitals were concerned mainly with the ethical implications of how research conducted under their auspices might affect patients; what is relatively new is the emergence of permanent structures dealing directly with everyday patient treatment issues. An ethicist might want to study specific case examples of ethical decision making by HECs, but the social science literature on HECs focuses on the process by which such decisions are made and the implications for both institutional structure and institutional culture that arise out of that process.

## SUGGESTIONS FOR FURTHER READING

A concise overview of the literature review and its place in the research process is provided by Martyn Hammersley (2004), "Literature Review" (p. 578) in *Encyclopedia of Social Science Research Methods*, edited by M. Lewis-Beck, A. E. Bryman, and T. F. Liao (Thousand Oaks, CA: Sage). There are also a number of online tutorials designed for college students who are learning the ropes of literature review. One that seems particularly user-friendly is provided by the library at American University in Washington DC. Its Web address is: www.library.american.edu/Help/tutorials/lit_review/index.html.

An excellent discussion of the skills required for choosing reputable Web sites for research is provided by Hope N. Tillman, "Evaluating Quality on the Net" (www.hopetillman.com/findqual.html). The Virginia Tech University libraries have put together a very useful Web site, "Bibliography on Evaluating Web Information" (www.lib.vt.edu/help/instruct/evaluate/evalbiblio.html) that includes documents addressing the issues related to critical use of Internet resources for research. Another good guide for using Internet resources and for determining the validity and reliability of those resources is "Using Internet Resources," published by the University of Toronto (www.erin.utoronto.ca/~w3lib/pub/evaluate/webevalu.htm).

Your campus library is the best place to start when it comes to finding out about databases relevant to your topic and problem. There are literally hundreds of databases on all manner of themes, and your reference librarian will be able to help you identify the ones that are readily accessible via your campus library computer network. For those of you interested in getting into the heavy-duty science of creating, managing, and using databases, the standard text is by C. J. Date (2003), *An Introduction to Database Systems, 8th ed.* (Reading, MA: Addison Wesley).

Some highlights of my own literature review discussed in this chapter include the following: Carol Taylor (1970), *In Horizontal Orbit: Hospitals and the Cult of Efficiency* (New York: Holt, Rinehart and Winston); Jack

Geiger (1975), "The Causes of Dehumanization in Health Care and Prospects for Humanization" (pp. 11–36) in *Humanizing Health Care*, edited by J. Howard and A. Strauss (New York: Wiley-Interscience); Ivan Illich (1976), *Medical Nemesis: The Expropriation of Health* (New York: Pantheon); Nathan Thornburgh (2006), "Teaching Doctors to Care," *Time* 167(22):58–59; John Stone and Richard Reynolds, eds. (2001), *On Doctoring: Stories, Poems, Essays, 3rd ed.* (New York: Simon and Schuster); Frances Norwood (2006), "The Ambivalent Chaplain: Negotiating Structural and Ideological Differences on the Margins of Modern-Day Hospital Medicine," *Medical Anthropology* 25(1):1–29; Elizabeth Heitman and Ruth Ellen Bulger (1998), "The Healthcare Ethics Committee in the Structural Transformation of Health Care: Administrative and Organizational Ethics in Changing Times," *Healthcare Ethics Committee Forum* 10(2):152–176; Terrence E. Deal and Allan A. Kennedy (1982), *Corporate Cultures: The Rites and Rituals of Corporate Life* (Harmondsworth: Penguin).

Check the Web site of the ACPE for links to documents, articles, and policy statements related to hospital chaplaincy.

## QUESTIONS FOR DISCUSSION

1. Conduct a literature review pertinent to the problem you identified in the last chapter. Write up an annotated bibliography of your most important sources.

2. Discuss the balance between primary and secondary sources in the literature you reviewed. Which ones came from traditional books and journals, and which were online resources? If you used established databases in your search, which ones were most helpful and how did you access them?

3. With regard to my own literature review, can you identify any aspects of hospital activity that might have been studied by social scientists that I neglected to include in my summary?

## NOTE

[1] Film buffs, however, may recall with amusement the exertions required of Julia Roberts in *Erin Brockovich* as the intrepid reporter tried to gain access to supposedly public records.

# Chapter Four

# Formulating Research Questions

———————◆—◆—————————

## You must next be able to *formulate one or more research questions* to guide your inquiry.

Formal experimental research is based on the testing of hypotheses—statements of precise relationships between or among variables that can be measured statistically. These relationships may take the form of a *null hypothesis* (the researcher predicts that there is no statistically significant relationship between or among the variables), a *nondirectional hypothesis* (the researcher predicts a relationship but chooses not to state what he or she thinks the direction of that relationship will be), or a *directional hypothesis* (the researcher states the direction of the relationship between the two variables, most often in the form "If X happens, then Y will follow").

Quantitative social research, which relies heavily on statistical analysis, aspires to the experimental hypothesis-testing model. It is therefore very important when planning a piece of quantitative research to make sure that one is indeed dealing with *variables*—factors that either induce change in other factors or that are themselves changed by the influence of others. One way to determine if you are working with a variable and not another kind of factor is to assess whether it is fact *measurable* and hence amenable to statistical analysis. For example, it is widely agreed that "stress" has something to do with health (or, more likely, illness). But "stress" is a very general concept that can mean many different things; it has many meanings in everyday discourse as well as in scientific parlance. In and of itself, then, "stress" is not really measurable. However, it is certainly possible to measure *perceived* stress by giving subjects a standardized questionnaire asking them to rate their own reactions to a set of common risk factors. Since stress is a very subjective matter, people who *think* they are under stress probably suffer the health consequences with greater regularity than those who are unaware of stressful aspects of their lives. So "perceived stress" is a measurable variable; it can serve as an *independent variable* that leads to a predicted change in another measurable variable (e.g., blood pressure), which would be the *dependent variable* in the formulation, "As a person's level of perceived stress increases, his or her blood pressure will also increase." Quantitative research favors the creation of measures before any data are collected, the better to standardize them. As a result, the data that are ultimately collected are primarily numerical in form and can be analyzed using statistics, tables, and charts.

Not all social research, however, lends itself to the hypothesis-testing model since there are often too many variables involved in the activities of groups with regard to a given social problem. Moreover, qualitative research is predicated on the researcher fitting into existing patterns of behavior rather than controlling the elements in a social situation. Under such circumstances, it is not possible to work from a hypothesis. It is, however, very important to work with one or more *research questions* that derive from your literature review in that it reflects what is known about a social issue and what needs to be investigated further. Just because qualitative research does not flow from formal hypotheses does not mean that it can be totally free-form; even "exploratory" research must be directed at the exploration of some defined field of activity.

A well-formed research question must be one that is answerable within the terms of a research project. For example, studies have shown that the suicide rate of college and university students in the United States is almost double that of their counterparts in Japan. It might be quite reasonable in the abstract to ask why. It would be logistically very difficult to obtain a representative sample of "college and university students in the United States" in the first place; moreover, you could not, by definition ask the students who committed suicide why they did so, and asking those who did not commit suicide why they did not could be an ethically untenable line of inquiry. So despite the superficial relevance of this question, it probably would not work as a research question after all. "There was a recent rash of suicides on the campus of Anywhere University; how did the students on that campus react to this situation?" would, on the other hand, be an answerable question that could shed indirect light on the larger, less easily answerable problem.

Rather than characterize their questions in terms of measurable variables, qualitative social researchers speak in terms of "concepts" that are played out in observations and interviews. You may not trust standardized measures of perceived stress, for example, but you can certainly explore the idea of stress by talking to people and by seeing how they behave in situations they regard as stressful. As a result, qualitative data most often take the form of words or images from documents, field notes, or transcripts. Analysis of such data involves finding themes in those words or images and organizing them into a thematically coherent, consistent overview.

A few basic guiding principles are good to keep in mind when devising research questions: (1) Do not lump too many different issues into one question. (2) Questions should not derive from background assumptions so complex or arcane that their point is obscure. (3) Questions should be phrased in terms of one of the classic journalistic queries (who, what, when, where, how?) rather than in terms of "why?" since you will want to establish the basic facts of the case before you try to figure out motives, attitudes, or values. (4) Questions should not be phrased in a way that suggests a controlled comparison between or among groups.

The process of defining variables so that a researcher (and his or her audience) will recognize them when they see them is known as *operationalization*. This process can be quite precise for quantitative researchers, since they can rely on standardized measures. Qualitative researchers, by contrast, are dealing with social factors that may not be measurable. But—and this point cannot be emphasized too strongly—that does not mean that qualitative researchers can work with ill-defined or vague ideas. Like classic hypotheses, the research questions of qualitative researchers should be phrased using precise statements that allow them (and their audiences) to understand just what it is they are looking for, and how everyone will know when that object of inquiry has been found.[1] Avoid using terms like "racism" or "social class," which over the years have accumulated so many different (and often conflicting) definitions that they have become, to all intents and purposes, meaningless. If you think that reactions to a rash of suicides will vary depending on the degree to which students feel "socially isolated," then it is incumbent on you to state exactly what you mean by that term, which is not at all self-evident, regardless of how frequently it is used in everyday discourse. For that matter, be clear what you mean by a "rash of suicides"—is this simply a journalistic exaggeration? How many cases constitute a "rash"?

The qualitative analogue to "operationalizing your variables" is stating very clearly what a term means. Even if it is a meaning that is idiosyncratic to you, you will not be confusing your audience if you tell them at the start what *your* definition is and if you are using that definition throughout your own processes of data collection and analysis, and then all the way through your published report. Even if your audience disagrees with your definition, they cannot then complain that they don't know what you're talking about. There are some forms of qualitative research (e.g., phenomenological inquiry) in which the researchers deliberately eschew any attempt at definitions; indeed in such research they are specifically instructed to "bracket" (i.e., set aside) any preconceived definitions they may have. The object of such research is to uncover the study subjects' own definitions. But in most cases, research can only be enhanced if you are able to see how your results fit into the existing body of knowledge, and you can only do so if you have clearly stated what it is you are looking for.

It is certainly possible to work with more than one research question; indeed, if you are working on a fairly complicated matter, it is preferable to break down your inquiry into several related questions rather than trying to compose a single, difficult-to-understand compound question. But unless you have the time and other resources to undertake a major research project, it is best to restrict yourself to one or two closely related questions.

# The Sample Project: Devising Research Questions

In developing my project, I established a general topical area: the moral/ethical dimension of health care in the contemporary United States. I then decided to concentrate on the ways in which hospitals, one of the key institutions of the health care system, have endeavored to adapt themselves to a climate based on compassionate care and "customer service." Since so many aspects of modern society have been "medicalized," as we noted in the commentary in chapter 1, it becomes increasingly important to understand how health care professionals—the gatekeepers to resources of institutionalized medicine—think of themselves and how they understand their roles in relationship to the general public. These issues lend themselves to an in-depth case study of one hospital. I further decided to frame the study as a work of applied social science (i.e., to include workable recommendations to the hospital as part of the analysis of the results). After reviewing the literature and reaching some conclusions about what is known about these matters, it was possible to state research questions that could guide the collection of data that would contribute to a satisfactory answer. My research questions were:

- How are the CGH pastoral care department and its HEC organized and how do they operate on a day-to-day basis?

- To what extent have they effected a change in the hospital's corporate culture? Are they integrated into the activities of the hospital's administration, staff, and patients?

As you can see, I have taken as my focus the two main structures identified in the literature as indicative of a shift in the corporate culture of hospitals from a "cult of efficiency" to an "ethic of caring": the pastoral care department and the hospital ethics committee. I am therefore asking first what these two entities actually do and second whether in fact they have effected a change in the corporate culture. Since "corporate culture" is a term that is not consistently defined in the literature, I operationalized it by stating that I would be looking to see if the presence and influence of pastoral care and the HEC are evident in both administrative policy and direct patient care (i.e., and not simply as rhetorical flourishes in the hospital's public relations announcements). In effect, I accepted what the literature suggests: that the values represented by both pastoral care and the HEC are at the core of an "ethic of caring." If those values have come to be a part of the everyday operations of the hospital, then I will assume that the "corporate culture" has indeed changed. Whatever else "corporate culture" may mean to other authors in other contexts, I will use it in the sense of a set of core values that guide both the policy and the day-to-day operations of a hospital.

Note that my questions do not assume that CGH is typical of anything other than itself. It is, however, the largest provider of health care in a large city, and its "corporate culture" is important in light of the major role CGH plays in the community. It would therefore be pertinent to see if it is in line with what the literature identifies as trends in hospital corporate culture. If it is, my recommendations might be offered as ways to strengthen or enhance this trend. If it is not, my recommendations might be offered as ways to bring it in line. In both instances, I began by assuming that CGH *wants* to be the sort of caring institution identified in the literature. If it does not, a follow-up research project might be in order— looking in a similarly in-depth way at other hospitals to see if CGH's rejection is part of a larger counter-trend or if it is an anomaly (and, if so, why is CGH the outrider?).

## SUGGESTIONS FOR FURTHER READING

Issues involved in the formulation of hypotheses and research questions, and the ins-and-outs of operationalization are explored in detail by P. D. Leedy (2001), *Practical Research: Planning and Design, 7th ed.* (Upper-Saddle River, NJ: Prentice-Hall). A more specifically qualitative treatment of these same matters is provided by Margaret D. LeCompte and Jean J. Schensul (1999), *Designing and Conducting Ethnographic Research* (Walnut Creek, CA: AltaMira).

## QUESTIONS FOR DISCUSSION

1. Formulate at least one, and no more than three, research question(s) about your proposed topic/problem based on what you have learned in your literature review. Be sure to provide clear operational definitions for all the terms in your questions. At this point do not assume that "everybody knows what each one means."

2. If you are planning to conduct a quantitative project, you may state your research question in the form of a hypothesis.

   a. Be sure to clearly identify your independent and dependent variables.

   b. Be sure to operationalize all your variables.

3. Take a careful look at my research questions. Are there aspects of life in a modern hospital that these questions implicitly exclude? How can such exclusions be justified?

## NOTE

[1] A Supreme Court justice once famously commented that he couldn't define pornography but that he knew it when he saw it. I am not competent to say whether this criterion meets legal standards, but it would not be a good basis for social research. A social scientist interested in "pornography" as a topic of research would have to define what he or she means by the term, since in the absence of a definition, the term could mean many different things to many different people.

# Chapter Five

# **Devising a Methodological Strategy**

---◆---

When you reach the fifth step,
you are ready to *choose a research method*
that is best suited to helping you answer
your research question(s).

Answering your research question(s) is a two-stage process. First, you must decide whether a quantitative or a qualitative *paradigm* (general framework) best suits your purposes *for a particular project*. You have probably already made this first decision back at the problem-defining stage, but now is the time to work out all the practical implications of that decision. Second, you must decide which data-collection techniques associated with one or the other of those paradigms will best help you reach a reasonable conclusion. It is usually a good idea to think in terms of two or three data-collection techniques so as to "triangulate" your conclusion—that is, reaching the same conclusion by several different means strengthens your claim to have come to that point in a trustworthy fashion. But it is usually a good idea to have the several data-collection techniques be ones associated with the same paradigm. Mixing quantitative and qualitative data collection in the same project can result in a good research product, particularly if the project is being conducted by multiple researchers. But for a single researcher, it is usually safer to stick with one paradigm, and then select data-collection techniques most clearly associated with that paradigm.

Quantitative research is, for the most part, based on the *deductive* process, which begins with an understanding of general processes and works down to an analysis of single cases within that general category. Qualitative research, by contrast, is *inductive*, which means that it operates by studying as many individual cases as come to hand and then building findings into a statement of a more general order. The deductive method allows quantitative researchers to determine the variables and categories of variables they want/need to study beforehand, since they will already have been established in general terms by prior research on the issue under study. The inductive method, however, leads qualitative researchers to build individual observations into categories as they go along. Qualitative research is therefore constantly evolving—the research design is rarely, if ever, pre-set as is the case with quantitative research as the collection of new information constantly changes the configuration of the general categories that will ultimately be used to analyze the entire situation.

# Data-Collection Techniques: Quantitative Research

Quantitative research by definition deals with numerical data. Researchers using this paradigm may conduct observations and interviews, which will be discussed in greater detail in the section on qualitative research, in the course of doing their experimental or hypothesis-testing inquiries, but they will always translate what they see and talk about into a form amenable to statistical analysis.

My students' favorite answer to the question, "How do they know that?" is, as mentioned earlier, the survey. Indeed, the survey is one of the principal data-collection techniques of social research and is typically associated with the quantitative rather than the qualitative pathway. Surveys are essentially tools for gathering information by having people ("respondents") answer a series of questions. Constructing an effective survey, however, means more than simply coming up with a list of questions.

The first step is to identify a target population. For example, you might be interested in finding out which factors lead college students to use on-campus health services. "College students" is thus a general target population. It is, however, clearly impossible to ask questions of every college student, so the next step is to select a sample composed of members of that target population who can be taken as representative of the larger group. A truly random sample is one in which respondents are selected in such a way that everyone in the target population has an equal chance of being included in the study. A random sample is desirable because it is the one most likely to yield results that are not the result of bias or other extraneous factors.

There are, however, any number of reasons why a truly random sample cannot be achieved. If, as in this example, your target population is "college students," then a random sample would necessarily include college students from all over the country (perhaps even all over the world). If you live in New York and true randomization ends up including respondents in Hawaii, and if you prefer to conduct face-to-face questioning rather than mailing, phoning, or e-mailing your survey (all of which have relatively low response rates), then this situation presents obvious barriers to the completion of your study. It is therefore sometimes necessary to use an "opportunistic" rather than a truly random sample—that is, one drawn randomly, but from a pool of potential respondents who are accessible, rather than ones who comprise the entire universe of potential respondents.

In some cases, the randomization process may be modified in favor of "stratification." A stratified sample is one that takes steps to make sure that certain sub-groups within the target population are represented. In such a sample, every member of the subgroup has an equal opportunity of being included. For example, in the hypothetical study involving college students, you might want to make sure that men and women, as well as members of particular ethnic groups, or people of certain religious traditions, or people with diverse majors are included in sufficient numbers, depending on what sorts of questions need to be asked.

Surveys distributed by phone, e-mail, or snail mail tend to produce low rates of response, as noted above, although they do have the advantage of allowing respondents to express their own ideas. Face-to-face interviews can sometimes be biased because respondents react to facial expressions or body language or other subtle cues that lead them to give the answer they think the researcher wants. Since both in-person and distance formats have drawbacks and benefits, it is up to the researcher to determine which situation best fits the constraints under which he or she is working.

Another matter that necessarily concerns the survey researcher is whether to frame questions in a closed format (e.g., multiple choice or other ways of limiting the possible answers) or an open-ended one (in which respondents answer in their own words). Again, there are pros and cons to each approach. Closed questions have the advantage of being easier to quantify and thus to analyze statistically, although they may limit the respondents, who might have to give the most nearly acceptable answer rather than the one they believe is actually correct. Open-ended questions allow greater personal expression, particularly when the matter under study is a subtle and complex one. Nevertheless, respondents' answers can be extremely difficult to summarize, since there is no guarantee that all respondents process ideas within the same set of categories for sorting out their thoughts.

When composing a survey, it is usually a good idea to begin with the most general, least threatening questions. It is therefore necessary to go into the study with at least a preliminary understanding of the group under study—what might be threatening to one population might be perfectly acceptable in another. It is also a good idea to try to get at the same information by using two or more questions worded somewhat differently, just to make sure that the respondent is being consistent and not giving haphazard, off the top-of-the-head answers. In all cases, questions should be clearly worded. Since researchers often speak a jargon-filled language of their own, it might be a good idea to pretest the survey by giving it to several trustworthy people who will not be part of the final sample and get their feedback as to the suitability and ease of comprehension of the questions. Each question should get at a single piece of information; avoid compound questions, or the kind of questions (beloved by professors composing essay exams) in which a lengthy explanatory discourse precedes the actual inquiry. It should also be obvious that if the survey needs to be administered in a language other than one you personally speak fluently, you should have it translated and then reviewed by people who are competent in that language.

# Data-Collection Techniques: Qualitative Research

In the quantitative paradigm, the essential approach to research involves hypothesis-testing, usually through some sort of experimental or survey design. The qualitative paradigm, by contrast, deals with research questions, which are more broadly defined than hypotheses, and it is therefore not surprising that this paradigm has spawned several distinct approaches to research, including the following.

- **Narrative analysis** is based on the collection of texts (spoken or written) that give accounts of an event or action. They are, in effect stories that people tell in order to encapsulate their experiences.

Such stories may be biographical (i.e., as told by an observer or interviewer) or autobiographical (i.e., as told by the person who lived through that event in his or her own words). When the story (or collection of related stories) comprises respondents' entire lives, it is called a "life history." When the story (or collection of related stories) focuses on recollections of a specific event, it is called an "oral history." A type of narrative that has come to prominence in recent years is the "testimonio," a story that is told with the specific intention of advocating for a particular social or political position. Stories may be generated firsthand by researchers who elicit them from people in the communities they study or they may be found in archival form (e.g., old letters collected by members of a family). In all cases, narrative analysis emphasizes the centrality of the individual and his or her experiences; in effect, society is seen as a mosaic of the experiences of its members.

- **Phenomenology**, which has its origins in several related schools of contemporary philosophy, is concerned with *meaning*. Although a phenomenological researcher works with narrative texts, his or her purpose is not to reconstruct either a personal life or a collective account of a shared event, but to discern what a particular "phenomenon" means to those who experience it. In most instances, the phenomenon is not a concrete event (such as "What we remember about 9/11," which would constitute an oral history) but is an attitude or an emotion (such as "terror"). Since we cannot take for granted that we understand such nonconcrete, albeit commonly used terms, the research is designed to probe how that term is used and what its usage conveys to those who experience a common set of circumstances.

- **Grounded theory** is meant to generate or discover a theory, an abstract analytical framework for understanding a social action. Proponents of this approach reject the notion that ways of understanding can derive from an outsider's academic perspective. They believe that understanding can only be valid if it reflects the perspectives of participants. Although related in some ways to phenomenology, grounded theory is concerned with explaining general categories of experience, rather than specific responses to a particular set of circumstances. A phenomenological study might begin with the question, "How do people who survived the collapse of the Twin Towers define 'terror'?" A grounded theory study would begin with the question, "How do people (i.e., not "experts") account for the rise of terrorism as a political tactic in the modern world?"

- **Ethnography**, which is sometimes used as a generic label for all qualitative field research, is a term best restricted to a study of a natural community, with the aim of providing a comprehensive descriptive portrait of life in that community at a particular moment in time.

- **Case study** is an approach that focuses on one aspect of life in a community. It is based on an in-depth study of a single setting in which that aspect can be seen with particular clarity, whereas an ethnography is concerned with getting the "big picture" of life in a community.

## Doing Research in the Qualitative Paradigm

Qualitative researchers can and do make use of some aspects of the survey research method, although they are more likely to work with one or another variant of three main skill sets: observation, interviewing, and the analysis of archival or secondary data. Although there are exceptions, qualitative researchers try to conduct their work in the "natural laboratory" of existing communities, a process referred to as "fieldwork." Moreover, they often strive to live in or, at least, spend a considerable amount of time in the communities they want to study. They are more or less active participants in the everyday lives of the people in their target populations rather than surveyors who are on the scene only in order to administer their questionnaires. Survey researchers, as we have seen, prefer to think of their data as objective, and so they want to maintain a distance between themselves and those they study. Qualitative researchers, by contrast, are content to embrace the subjective nature of reality; they believe that becoming part of the group enhances their ability to understand what is going on, even if doing so means that they might be influencing the reactions of the other members of the group.

When fieldworkers interact directly for an extended period of time in their study communities, they are conducting research by means of "participant observation." For example, to return to the research proposed above, a qualitative researcher based on a particular college campus might choose to do participant observation on that campus, drawing on his or her personal knowledge of that campus community and his or her existing relationships with its citizens. He or she must, however, carefully note the ways in which that campus is and is not typical of campuses elsewhere; that campus study might yield some suggestions about larger trends, but it cannot be seen as truly representative of anything beyond itself. It should, however, be kept in mind that participant observation is not a data-collection method per se, but the context in which other methods can be deployed.

## Observation

Observation is the act of perceiving the activities and interrelationships of people in the community under study through the five senses of the researcher. It is very important for fieldworkers to remember that their senses can be deceived. In fact, we all go through life perceiving things through filters—our preconceived notions of how things are. We are usually not conscious of the ways in which our cultural backgrounds, social class affiliations, gender, and so forth lead us to view the world in certain ways, but in fact we are always making such *ethnocentric* judgments. A good fieldworker must therefore be conscious of these sources of potential bias and strive to set them aside. At the very least, the potential biasing factors should be acknowledged so that readers of the research report can judge for themselves whether the researcher is a trustworthy guide to what is going on in the community under study.

It is sometimes said that a fieldworker should ideally become like a little child when in the field in the sense that a child takes nothing for granted; in effect, everything is new to both the child and the field-working observer. The formal process of research observation begins by taking everything in and recording it in meticulous detail, avoiding interpretation as much as possible. For example, one should note that "The people in the temple were chanting and swaying to the beat of a drum," rather than "The people in the temple were carried away by religious ecstasy." The latter inference might well turn out to be true, but you should avoid leaping to such a conclusion before you have a solid grasp of what is actually going on.

As the observer gains more experience in the community, he or she may begin to discern matters that seem to be particularly important (e.g., because they are repeated with some frequency, or because people seem to be paying more careful attention when they happen); he or she may thus begin to focus on these matters, filtering out extraneous material. In our everyday lives, of course, we do this automatically—we learn to ignore all sorts of "background noise" in our environments. Imagine how quickly we would be overwhelmed if we tried to pay attention to *everything* all the time! The difference in fieldwork, however, is that we are gradually learning to take on the local people's filters rather than rely on our own. We are learning to perceive the world in terms of what they, not we, think is important. Doing so may be relatively easy when the field-work is being conducted in obviously "exotic" settings, so different from our own that we know how foolish it would be to try to see the world through the lens of our own culture. The process is much more difficult in those settings that seem superficially very much like our own. They may well turn out to be similar in ways that will eventually allow us to use our own navigational skills to understand them. But we cannot start out at that point.

Some observational techniques are said to be *unobtrusive,* which means that those being studied do not know that they are being observed. Modern standards of ethical research, however, emphasize the principle of "informed consent," which has made truly unobtrusive observation unacceptable except in settings that are public and where no one has the obligation to introduce himself or herself (e.g., airport waiting lounges). In most participant observational settings, however, it would be highly unethical for someone who is actively participating in a community to be conducting observations for his or her research without informing the people and giving them the option to remove themselves from the research. Participant observers must also decide the extent to which they want to be members of the communities they study. They should also consider the extent to which members of the community will expect them to become members of the group.

Because qualitative research is conducted in the a "natural" field set-ting over which researchers have little or no control, it is very important that they choose a research site that will allow them to answer the research questions that are at the center of the project. *Site selection* is thus their first task. This process begins with a personal inventory: think about your own emotions, attitudes, values, and preferences. What kinds of peo-ple or situations are you comfortable with? What kinds of people or situa-tions are you unfamiliar with but are eager to challenge yourself with? What kinds of people or situations are you unwilling to deal with at all?

Do not be ashamed about having such preferences—there is no point in forcing yourself to be miserable just because you think that a good researcher should be able to fit in anywhere. If you are uncomfortable, you will not do good research, no matter how fine your technical skills may be. If you come to the conclusion that the research questions you have posed can be answered *only* in a setting in which you are sure you cannot func-tion, then come up with different questions that can be dealt with in a more comfortable setting. Doing so is not an admission of defeat; being able to do good research is a winning proposition for all concerned. It is sometimes the case that even with careful thought and preparation, researchers finds themselves in field settings that really aren't personally satisfying. There is nothing wrong with withdrawing and starting over, as long as you are not cutting and running at the first sign of difficulty.

When doing this personal inventory, consider not only whether factors in the possible community are comfortable for you; but think also of whether *you* will be comfortable for the people in the community. You may, for example, be a man with a firm commitment to gender equality and a genuine sensitivity to contemporary women's issues. But trying to do field research in a support group for female rape survivors may not work out—your gender (and its perceived attributes) might get in the way of your research. It goes without saying that all the readers of this book are wonderful, generous, outgoing, lovable people who would be welcome in communities around the world. But just in case anyone has doubts about his or her ability to fit in, a few pointers may be in order.

- Don't assume that communities closer to home or with cultures similar to your own will be easier to fit into.

- By the same token, don't assume that in a community like your own you already know everything there is to know about fitting in.

- Do not allow yourself to be "captured" by the first people who make you feel welcome. You need to select a community in which you can reasonably maintain a friendly, but not overly eager distance until you have a good idea of what is going on. Researchers doing fieldwork in religious congregations, for example, are often assumed to be prime candidates for conversion, so if you think you will be unable to explain your purposes to a group of zealots, think twice about working with that group.

- Unless you are doing purely unobtrusive observational research, think about how you can be helpful to the members of the group once you have established yourself as a participant observer. People are often surprisingly willing to tolerate your presence just to be polite, but they will be much happier to work with you on your research if they know you are willing to pitch in to help them achieve some of their own goals. It should be obvious that if their goals involve criminal activity (or any other activities that you find unacceptable) you will not fit in.

- Make sure that what you know beforehand about the community's social conventions lead you to think that you can be respectful of their values and attitudes, which does not necessarily mean that you have to agree with or share all of those values and attitudes.

In sum, do not choose a field site in which *you* become the object of discussion and contention.

Once you have decided on a field setting that seems comfortable both for you and for the people in the community, you may want to keep the following points in mind.

- Select a site in which the issue you are exploring is most likely to be observed (e.g., if your research questions have to do with people's reactions to urban renewal programs, then don't choose a rural setting just because you personally prefer spending time in the country).

- Select a site that is comparable to others that have been studied by other researchers, but not one that has been overstudied.[1]

- Select a site with a minimum of gatekeeping obstacles. Gatekeepers are people or institutions in a community that set up and enforce regulations about who can enter the community and what they can do when they get there. Some gatekeepers function in the name of formal authority (e.g., the police, the administrative staff of an institution like a hospital or a school), while others are informal (e.g., the patriarch of a community based on traditional family ties). It is up to you to decide when the gatekeepers' requirements become more burdensome than they are worth to you to do your research.[2]

- Select a site in which you will not be more of a burden than you are worth to the community (e.g., do not think of doing a study in a hospital emergency room in which you mainly stand around observing; you will simply be in the way).

If it is to be useful for research, observation—whether unobtrusive or participant-based—must be rendered in the form of organized notes, since few people are blessed with photographic memories for all the details and nuances that cross their field of perception over the course of a project. Field notes should include:

- a statement about the particular setting in which the observation occurred—if the entire project took place in a hospital, then it is necessary to specify which unit or department of the hospital was the site of the particular observation;

- a general categorization of the participants (How many people were involved? What were their general characteristics with regard to age, gender, and other relevant categories?);

- a description of the participants, rendered in as nearly objective a form as possible (e.g., "The man wore a torn, dirty pair of pants," not "The man looked poor");

- a chronology of events;

- descriptions of the physical setting and all material objects involved; especially at the beginning, assume nothing (e.g., you might think that an observation in a hospital room would "of course" involve a bed, but hospital beds are not like beds at home, nor are they always arranged in the same way, depending on the particular needs of the patient or the requirements of the nursing staff in a particular unit; in any case, just saying that there was a bed in the room is not very informative);

- descriptions of behaviors and interactions, again avoiding interpretations (e.g, "The man was weeping and repeatedly struck his head with his fist," not "The man was distraught");

- records of verbal interactions that you overhear (as near to verbatim as possible, particularly if it is not feasible or desirable to have a tape recorder on hand)—remember that at this point you are not interviewing anyone, so these overheard conversations are not ones that you initiate or control.

One final note on notes: it really doesn't matter which medium you use to record your notes. Most fieldworkers nowadays like to enter their notes directly onto their laptops; there are even software programs to facilitate this process. Others prefer more old-fashioned manual methods (e.g., index cards, loose-leaf notebooks). What is important is that *you* (the primary user of those notes) will be able to retrieve the information in an efficient fashion. Since you will certainly want to protect the anonymity of your research subjects, the format you choose should allow you to devise a way to code the information so that unauthorized viewers will not be able to identify anyone. Some observational researchers are increasingly relying on video records, particularly as video recording equipment is now readily available and reasonably inexpensive. There are, however, many ethical problems with video recordings of field "notes," and extra precautions must be taken to preserve the privacy of those involved in the study.

## Interviewing

Interviewing is a process of directing a conversation so as to collect information. As noted above, observation ultimately leads a researcher to the discernment of patterns in behaviors and interactions. The inevitable next question is: what do those behaviors mean to the people who are involved in the research setting? It is therefore necessary at that point to ask questions. Sometimes we question people who have expert knowledge about the community (*key informants*); at other times we question people who give us the "common knowledge" perspective. In either case, interviewing in the field grows naturally out of observation.

Just as observation for research purposes requires organizing and regularizing processes that are part of our everyday lives, so too is research-interviewing a careful extension of ordinary conversation. Interviewing in the field is certainly conversational in the sense that it takes place between people who have grown to be friendly with one another, but it needs to go beyond the free-form conversation of friends, since the researcher needs to find out certain things and must be vigilant in keeping the conversation on track—and must, moreover, do so without seeming to be coercive or impatient.

The field interview is therefore typically *open-ended* in nature in that it flows with conversational rhythms and accommodates digressions, which may well open up new avenues of inquiry that the researcher had not originally considered. In that sense it is a partnership in which the informed insider helps the researcher develop the inquiry as it goes along. The field interview is also conducted *in depth*. It is not merely an oral version of a survey questionnaire. Instead, it is intended to probe for meaning, to explore nuances, to capture the gray areas that might be missed in either/or questions that merely suggest the surface of an issue.

It is true that interviews in the field sometimes happen spontaneously, but they are most effective when the researcher has prepared for them and has arranged a time that is convenient for both parties, so that both the interviewer and the interviewee can concentrate on the task at hand. Preparation for the interview should involve deciding on a topical or thematic focus. Telling someone "I want to talk to you about life on this campus" is not very helpful either to you or to the person you are interviewing. "I want to talk to you about the kinds of clubs a student can join on this campus" is more likely to yield meaningful results.

Be careful about plunging into controversial or sensitive issues with people you don't know very well; you may not be able to anticipate everything that a potential interviewee will or will not think is sensitive, but doing your homework should allow you to identify potential sources of discomfort. Your preparation should therefore involve reviewing everything you know (or think you know) about the topic. Doing so will also allow you to come up with a few possible questions to get the ball rolling; do not, however, stick doggedly to that set of questions, lest you come off like a news reporter or, even worse, a police officer grilling a suspect. Interviewees more often than not try to be helpful, but they do not always know what you are looking for. If a response does not get at information that you think is important, you will have to go beyond the generic questions and ask some probing questions, which might entail:

- repeating what the person has said, but rephrasing it as a question to make sure that you have understood correctly ("So you moved to this neighborhood because you thought the public schools were especially good?");

- asking for specific information ("You mentioned that you liked the campus health clinic. What sort of services does it provide?");

- asking for clarification of apparent contradictions ("You said that you liked the campus health clinic because it is open even on holidays, but you went to the hospital ER when you got sick on Thanksgiving. Why was that?");

- asking for an opinion ("Do you think that the campus health clinic is adequately supported in the university's budget?");

- asking for clarification of a term or a complex process;[3]

- requesting *narratives of experience* (i.e., concrete anecdotes that illustrate a general point)—nothing brings a research report to life more effectively than the actual words, reflecting the actual experiences, of participants.

In addition to these positive steps that you can take to make an interview work, there are several things to avoid, things that might add up to *interviewer bias:*

- Do not ask leading questions that essentially tell the interviewee the answer you are expecting ("Shouldn't all the students enthusiastically support the campus health clinic?").

- Do not ignore leads when the interviewee introduces new themes that seem important to him or her.

- Do not redirect or interrupt a story.

- Do not ignore the interviewee's nonverbal cues (e.g., signs of boredom, anger, or irritation).

- Do not use nonverbal cues to indicate that you think a response was "right" or "wrong."

In addition to specific techniques that keep the interview flowing, there are several points that speak to the overall "etiquette" of conducting an interview.

- Make sure the interview takes place in a setting that is convenient and comfortable for both of you.

- Spend some time in ice-breaking small talk.

- Maintain good eye contact.

- Try to avoid injecting yourself too much into the narrative; it is fine to offer your own opinions and perspectives, as long as you do not turn the interview into *your* story.

- Be aware of the condition of the person you are interviewing (i.e., do not overtax those who are in frail health, or insist that someone with mental challenges deal with very complex issues).

- Personalize the interview (e.g., ask the person to share photos or other memorabilia that bring the subject matter to life).

Students often ask, "How many interviews do I need to do?" There is, alas, no definitive answer to that question. One response might be that the size of the sample depends on the characteristics of the community being studied, on your own resources (i.e., limitations of time, mobility, access to recording equipment), and on the objectives of your study. If your study community is diverse, then you will need to interview and observe more people in order to be sure that you have a good overview of all the different elements within the group. In a more nearly homogeneous group, you may be able to assume that one or two people will reflect the views and experiences of everyone.

Interviews are typically recorded on audiotape, which is a way of assuring the accuracy of what was said. Audio taping, however, requires a fair amount of equipment (a recorder, possibly an external microphone, blank tapes, working batteries or an electrical converter) that may not always be comfortable or convenient to tote around. (Lugging and setting up recording equipment in the room of a hospital patient might make it difficult to establish rapport.) Consider what your *essential* needs are—do not commit yourself to a load of complicated equipment unless excellent sound reproduction is an intrinsic part of the study, as might be the case if you are interviewing musicians about their performance techniques.

It is possible to buy reasonably inexpensive and more or less unobtrusive recorders adequate for most research situations. However, with any type of equipment, you will end up with "tapes" (I am using this old-fan-

gled term in a generic sense to include digital media on which contemporary recordings may be made) that need to be indexed and possibly
transcribed so that you can easily access the material. Keep in mind that,
at best, transcription is a slow, tedious process that researchers often have
neither the time nor the skill to do properly. On the other hand, the services of a professional transcriber can price a project out of the ballpark. It
is therefore important to be attuned to what you can do for yourself and
how much you can afford to pay others to help you; such calculations will
determine how many interviews you end up doing.

## Archival and/or Secondary Research

It should be noted that although I am using "archival" and "secondary" data as synonyms, there are social scientists who prefer to restrict the
latter term to material (either quantified or narrative in form) that has
been collected *by other researchers* for projects of their own but are available
to later researchers, who can re-analyze it for their own purposes. My
only reason for lumping them together is because they are not the products of a researcher's own firsthand inquiry, instead they are existing
resources that are available for repurposing.

Archival/secondary research relies on the analysis of materials that
have been stored for both official and unofficial purposes. Official records
(e.g., maps; records of births, deaths, marriages, real estate transactions;
census, tax, and voting rolls; transcripts of court proceedings; minutes of
meetings; publications prepared and distributed by public agencies) are
usually available to the public and are increasingly available online,
although some may require special permission for access. The data contained in official records tend to be well organized and retained in a format that enables efficient, easy handling. However, some forms of
recorded material, such as original copies of old newspapers or maga-
zines, can be difficult to handle and read. Fortunately, many of them have
been digitized, making them easy to use. But we cannot rely on such a
process across the board, and there are undoubtedly many such sources
that exist only in their original physical form, with its tendency to decay,
or even be destroyed outright.

Unofficial records, such as a family's collection of memorabilia, may
not be well organized at all, and even with permission to access them,
they may not be conveniently located or in a state of preservation that
makes for ease of using them for research. Despite such potential problems, archived data (even when the "archivist" has merely thrown stuff

into a carton in his basement) can be an interesting source of information. When the data are in statistical form, they can be helpful to the quantitative researcher, who can thus trace trends and patterns through time. When they are in narrative form (such as with stories in newspapers), or in the form of objects whose narrative needs to be unraveled, they are more likely the province of qualitative researchers.

Archival research rarely stands alone as a data-collection technique, although it can certainly be the basis of a respectable stand-alone study if firsthand fieldwork is not feasible. But accessing and (re)interpreting archived or secondary materials is almost always facilitated when the researcher has firsthand experience in the community under study, and when he or she can check inferences made from the archived data in interviews with currently active members of that community.

There are several advantages to using archival or secondary materials in a social research project:

- It is generally nonreactive. That is, the researcher cannot influence people's responses, since he or she is not interacting directly with the people who provided the information in the first place.

- It is usually relatively inexpensive (although, depending on where the archived material is stored, there may be travel expenses involved—a factor mitigated when the material is available online).

- It is especially useful when one is interested in studying changing events, behaviors, or attitudes over the course of time.

- It is also valuable when studying topics that might be considered too sensitive or volatile to observe or ask questions about directly.

On the other hand, a researcher using archived material should be aware of some potential problems:

- Such data are not always unbiased. Who collected the material? For what purposes? What might have been left out (intentionally or otherwise) in the collection process? Every collection is the result of a process of editorial selection; the researcher who comes along later is therefore not dealing with "pure" information.

- Even computerized databases are not always free of error; just because the information has been carefully transcribed does not mean that it was accurate to begin with.

- There can be physical or logistical problems in working with these data, which may be stored in inconvenient or physically unattractive (dusty, dirty, rat- or roach-infested) places.

Despite such caveats, however, archived materials are simply too rich a resource to be ignored.

# Methods for the Sample Project

Decisions made at earlier points of the process have led me to choose a qualitative paradigm with a case study approach. The designated site of my case study was the place I have called City General Hospital (CGH), to which I already had access as a member of a community advisory board whose deliberations had stimulated my thinking about a particular issue (the evolution of an "ethic of care"). Moreover, other members of the board encouraged me to develop a research project at the hospital. Since my findings would be directed to the institution itself in the interest of helping it refine its procedures, so as to carry out its new corporate mission, the study would be applied in nature.

It would certainly be possible to do the CGH case study solely by using archival and secondary data. A hospital generates a great deal of information about itself in the form of internal memos, publicity given out to the public, and reports to accrediting agencies. As a public hospital in a state with a "sunshine law" (which mandates that the records of public agencies be available to the public even if, like minutes of meetings, they were not originally generated for public consumption), CGH would be obliged to make its records available to a researcher. Moreover, as a member of the community board I would be in a position to expedite the retrieval of those records. I am, however, a cultural anthropologist by training, and all of my professional instincts lead me to prefer to conduct research in the context of participant observation in the field setting. The archived materials could certainly be used, but I also wanted to get a first-hand look at what was going on in the hospital and to talk directly to those involved in the implementation of the "ethic of caring" mission.

Wanting to do participant observation-based research is one thing; being able to do so is quite another. Hospitals have especially elaborate gatekeeping structures, since they must be vigilant in protecting the safety and privacy of patients and since they must make sure that the complex and delicate procedures being carried out by doctors, nurses, technicians, and other staff are not compromised by those who are not directly contributing to the care of the patients. Conducting observations in a hospital is not like conducting observations in a public park or an airport waiting room. Many hospitals (although not CGH at the time of my study) even require people visiting patients to have a special visitor pass in order to go beyond the main lobby. Moreover, hospital staff are not easily coaxed into sitting for interviews, in some cases because of their concern for patient privacy, in other cases because health care professionals are simply not used to being questioned by laypeople about what they do. My role as a board member did give me an entrée, but in that role I would still be only an unhelpful body in the way of staff members going about their business of treating sick people.

I therefore decided that I needed to take on a more active "membership role" at the hospital. Since my research questions were leading me to a particularly close examination of the religious ministries service of the hospital, I decided to enroll in a unit of Clinical Pastoral Education (CPE), the training course mandated for those who work as hospital chaplains. Clergy from the community may visit members of their congregations who are patients at the hospital without additional credentials; chaplains who are employed by the hospital need CPE credentials whether or not they are ordained clergy. I am not ordained, but my CPE credentials allowed me to become a staff member of the CGH pastoral care department as a "chaplain intern" (unpaid). In that capacity, I was able to move freely around the hospital and was acknowledged as being able to carry out recognized and useful functions. I could, for example, remain in the emergency room when an ambulance brought in a trauma case since I could offer assistance to the patient and his or her family; without being a "chaplain intern" I would have been politely but very firmly asked to step outside.

I spent six months as a participant observer at CGH—a chaplain intern who was also conducting research. I conducted observations in all units of the hospital, shadowed the full-time professional hospital chaplains on their rounds, attended meetings of the HEC, participated in orientations for new staff, and was granted access to a wide variety of archived records. I was therefore able to come up with a comprehensive picture of life at CGH at a particular moment in time and to see the "culture of caring" in operation, as it was lived rather than simply as how it was envisioned in the corporate literature.

## SUGGESTIONS FOR FURTHER READING

The standard study of research design in qualitative social research is John W. Creswell (2007), *Qualitative Inquiry and Research Design: Choosing among Five Approaches* (Thousand Oaks, CA: Sage). Uwe Flick's (2007) *Designing Qualitative* Research (London: Sage) is a useful digest of that same information. Creswell's (1994) *Research Design: Qualitative and Quantitative Approaches* (Thousand Oaks, CA: Sage) is an excellent comparative introduction to the two paradigms. The most frequently cited source for the case study approach is R. K. Yin (1994), *Case Study Research: Design and Methods* (Beverly Hills, CA: Sage).

The many forms and uses of observation in social science, both past and present, are treated by Patricia A. Adler and Peter Adler (1994), "Observational Techniques" (pp. 377–392) in *Handbook of Qualitative Research*, edited by N. K. Denzin and Y. S. Lincoln (Thousand Oaks, CA: Sage); Michael Angrosino and Kimberly Mays de Pérez (2000), "Rethinking Observation: From Method to Context" (pp. 673–702) in *Handbook of Qualitative Research, 2nd ed.,* edited by N. K. Denzin and Y. S. Lincoln (Thousand Oaks, CA: Sage; Michael Angrosino, "Recontextualizing Observation: Ethnography, Pedagogy, and the Prospects for a Progressive Political Agenda" (pp. 729–746) in *Handbook of Qualitative Research, 3rd ed.,* edited by N. Denzin and Y. S. Lincoln (Thousand Oaks, CA: Sage); Michael Angrosino (2007), *Doing Ethnographic and Observational Research* (London: Sage); and Michael Angrosino (2007), *Naturalistic Observation* (Walnut Creek, CA: LeftCoast). For some practical pointers, consult Gerry Tierney (2007), "Becoming a Participant Observer" (pp. 9–18) in *Doing Cultural Anthropology, 2nd ed.,* edited by Michael Angrosino (Long Grove, IL: Waveland Press) and Laurie Price (2007), "Carrying Out a Structured Observation" (pp. 91–98) in *Doing Cultural Anthropology, 2nd ed.,* edited by Michael Angrosino (Long Grove, IL: Waveland Press). A variety of social scientists tell personal stories about doing participant observation-based research in a volume edited by Lynne Hume and Jane Mulcock (2004), *Anthropologists in the Field: Cases in Participant Observation* (New York: Columbia University Press).

The art of interviewing is reviewed in detail by Steinar Kvale (2007), *Doing Interviews* (London: Sage).

Archival research is covered by E. Webb, D. T. Campbell, R. D. Schwartz, L. Sechrest, and J. B. Grove (1981), *Nonreactive Measures in the Social Sciences* (Boston: Houghton Mifflin).

Stephen L. Schensul, Jean J. Schensul, and Margaret D. LeCompte (1999), *Essential Ethnographic Methods: Observations, Interviews, and Questionnaires* (Walnut Creek, CA: AltaMira) is a comprehensive and in-depth look at these key data-collection techniques.

## QUESTIONS FOR DISCUSSION

1. Given the research questions you have formulated, select a *paradigm* (quantitative or qualitative) that will be the framework for your research. Clearly explain and justify your choice.

    a. Select an *approach* that fits your paradigm (e.g., experiment or field survey for quantitative, ethnography, case study, narrative analysis, phenomenology, grounded theory for qualitative). Clearly explain and justify your choice.

    b. Select one or more data-collection techniques that fits your approach. Clearly explain and justify your choice.

2. If you are proposing to do a field study, indicate the site(s) for the research. Explain and justify your choice. If the site(s) poses significant gatekeeping issues, explain how you will deal with them.

3. If your field study will involve *participant* observation, explain what role you propose to play and discuss how you will explain yourself to the people at your field site.

4. If your study will involve the administration of a survey, draft a version of your questionnaire and give it to people you think will have a grasp of the issues you are studying *but who will not be part of your research sample.* Get their feedback: were the questions worded clearly? Did the survey take too long to answer? Were the questions too insensitive?

5. Get together with a group from your class and go to some public place on your campus. Each of you should conduct a nonparticipant observation of that place without consulting with each other. Compare and contrast the results. Did you all come up with the same description? If not, which elements were common, and which ones reflected individual perspectives? On the whole, what level of descriptive detail seems most satisfying to the group?

6. Pair up with another student from your class to practice interviewing. You should each take a turn as the interviewer and a turn as the interviewee. Pick a topic that both of you are interested in and have some knowledge about, but don't be too concerned about the content—focus rather on the technique of the interview. Give each other an honest critique. If time and resources permit, you may record these sample interviews (audio- or videotape) and show them to your instructor and/or the rest of the class for their comments. In

sum, what do you think *your* best assets are as an interviewer? What are your weak points and how might you overcome them?

7. Discuss the pros and cons of the decisions I made about being a credentialed (albeit temporary) member of the hospital staff in order to conduct my research on-site.

## NOTES

[1] A joke from my graduate school days had it that the typical Navajo family consists of a mother, a father, three children, and an anthropologist.

[2] As we will see in later chapters, would-be hospital researchers must negotiate a veritable phalanx of gatekeepers. Given the nature of the issues I set out to research, I had no choice but to deal with them. My suggestion, though, is that if you don't absolutely *have* to work in a gatekeeper-intensive site, then by all means go somewhere else.

[3] We each have gaps in our knowledge; if the person you are interviewing gets into matters that you don't understand, don't hesitate to ask for explanations. It can be taken as a given that you have asked the person to sit for an interview because he or she is an expert on a topic that you presumably know less about; if you were already all-knowing, why bother with an interview? You will not seem ignorant or foolish if you ask the person to clarify something that might be perfectly obvious to him or her.

# Chapter Six

# Collecting Data

――――◆◆◆――――

The sixth step is to **collect your data**.

Once you have decided on an overall research method and specific data-collection techniques, you can proceed to gather the information you need in order to answer your question. The act of collection should always be conducted with two very important ideas in mind. First, consider the *validity* of the data. This criterion means that your operational definitions are actually measuring what they are supposed to measure. As you go along, particularly in ethnographic research, you may have to refine your operational definitions as you learn more about the situation as it is really acted out, just so there will be no guesswork about what you are looking for. Second, you must be mindful of the *reliability* of the data, which means that if other researchers used your operational definitions to answer your research questions they would come up with findings that were consistent with yours. The entire data-collection process should involve you in an ongoing critical examination of the validity and the reliability of the data you are collecting.

# Research Ethics

We have already mentioned ethical considerations that play an important role in conducting social research. Since attention to the ethical dimension of research is a required part of any contemporary proposal for research, it is as much a part of the planning as the formulation of research questions and the selection of a research design and appropriate data-collection techniques. We therefore need to take a closer look at the ethical dimension of social research. Since most ethical issues arise in the context of data collection, however, it seems appropriate to discuss these factors in this chapter—with the caution that they should be taken into consideration before and after, as well as during the data-collection phase.

All social research involves researchers coming into contact with other human beings whom they are studying. In the case of experimental or survey research, the contact may seem to be distant, whereas in field-work (particularly the participant observation variety thereof) it may seem to be much closer. In reality, any kind of human contact raises ethical issues that have come to the fore in the minds of researchers in recent decades. One simply cannot discuss the techniques of data collection without also discussing the ethical dimension of that research.

There are three levels on which ethical considerations bear on the conduct of research:

1. The official, published standards mandated by the government; they are operative in most universities and other research institutions that receive government funding

2. Codes of ethics promulgated by professional societies to which researchers belong

3. Our own personal values, which may be the product of our religious traditions, the consensus within our peer group, our own personal reflection on issues of concern, or some combination of all these factors

## Official Standards and Institutional Structures

Social research is governed by a structure of institutional review boards (IRBs), which, since the 1960s, have grown out of federal regulations mandating *informed consent* from all those participating in federally funded research. In the regulatory language, such participants are referred to as "human subjects." The protection of those human subjects became an issue as a number of research projects (mostly biomedical experiments) led to the injury or even death of participants. In order to save subjects from the negative effects of "intrusive" research, participation in a research project was made to be a choice that the potential subjects could control. In order for them to make a reasonable choice, they need to be informed about the nature of the project and the procedures it entails.

This process is not dissimilar to the informed consent a patient in a hospital would be asked to sign, indicating that he or she has been told about what a recommended procedure or therapeutic regimen will entail and what its possible side effects might be. By signing, the patient agrees to the procedure, fully informed about both the benefits and the risks involved. So too, a potential research subject, by signing an informed consent form, agrees to participate, fully informed about the aims and procedures of the research, as well as its potential benefits and risks to the subject (and, if applicable, to the community to which he or she belongs).

In biomedical research, the most important goal is to protect subjects from physical harm and/or psychological injury. In social research, there is also a major concern with safeguarding the privacy of human subjects and maintaining the confidentiality of all records that might identify them. Although we cannot presume to know what matters, potential subjects will want to be kept confidential, researchers must proceed carefully to take into account personal and community norms regarding sensitive matters, and then take appropriate steps to assure that anything deemed sensitive will be protected. One common way to protect privacy and ensure confidentiality is to use codes—numbers or pseudonyms—when describing people in field notes and in any reports generated by the research. The researcher can also make sure that his or her notes will be kept in a secure place, or that they will be destroyed upon completion of the project. Copies of research records (e.g., tapes and/or transcripts of interviews) could be returned to the subjects for approval prior to publication of any product based on those records.

Unlike clergy, physicians, or attorneys, researchers do not enjoy an automatic privilege of confidentiality recognized by the law.[1] In the worst case scenario, our promise to protect a subject's confidentiality cannot withstand a court subpoena. We can do our best to protect our sources, but like journalists, we must be prepared to pay the consequences should we opt to ignore a subpoena.

The establishment of the IRB structure was a logical outgrowth of the articulation of the right to informed consent. An IRB is essentially a committee composed of experienced researchers and legal experts affiliated with a university or research institution; they review proposals submitted by members of their faculties and student bodies to make sure that adequate precautions have been taken to provide for informed consent and to protect the privacy and confidentiality of human subjects. Proposals that do not pass muster with the IRB cannot be carried out, lest the university incur federal punishment (e.g., withholding of funds). Many universities have adopted a dual IRB system—one for biomedical research and one for social and behavioral research. It should be noted, however, that the latter is often dominated by psychologists, who tend to adhere to a bio-medically influenced experimental model of research. Because they are often in a position to control all the variables in their research settings, they do not always understand the special needs of social researchers, especially qualitative fieldworkers, who truly cannot anticipate everything that might happen in a "natural" setting.

No qualitative researcher would seriously argue against the need for an ethical review structure, but there is a perceived need to educate IRBs to the nuanced diversity of research and the possible different strategies that can be deployed to ensure privacy and confidentiality. One solution adopted at many universities is to provide for an "expedited" review of projects that seem to have minimal potential for doing harm (a subjective judgment, at best); some also provide for an "exempt" category, which might include projects that rely almost exclusively on archived materials already on the public record or on observations conducted unobtrusively in public places where people have no expectation of privacy (campus cafeteria OK, campus restroom not OK). Since most qualitative research will ultimately involve observations that cannot be conducted unobtrusively, not to mention face-to-face interviews, the likelihood of coming up with a project that is truly exempt is very small. In any case, any project involving designated *vulnerable populations* (children, people with diminished mental capacity, people in jail) must receive very rigorous review.

Rules governing projects conducted by students as class assignments are inconsistent, so it is always best to have your instructor check with your school's IRB to see if projects developed as part of a class, such as that suggested by this book, must be reviewed. If so, it will be necessary to factor the review time into the research process, since you cannot ethically begin the research until the IRB gives its approval. Student research that is not part of a class assignment (e.g., an independent honors project, a master's or doctoral research project) falls into the same category as regular faculty research.

## Codes of Ethics

The ethics statement promulgated by the American Anthropological Association (AAA) may be taken as representative of those that are in use in most of the social sciences. According to the AAA, researchers must be open about the purpose, potential impact, and source of support for their project as they propose and then carry out their research. The *primary* responsibility of researchers is to the *people with whom they work and whose lives and cultures they study.* (You will note that the AAA, like most social science associations, rejects the governmental/bureaucratic language of "human subjects," which sounds "experimental" in all the worst ways.) In effect, researchers' responsibilities to the scientific community and to the general public (the potential consumers of the products of their research) are important, but always secondary to their responsibility to the study population. The AAA makes it clear that researchers should strive to be ethical, regardless of whether their project is "basic," "applied," or "proprietary" in nature. (Proprietary research is that which is conducted in and on behalf of a particular agency that has contracted with the researcher to maintain ownership rights over the research product.)

## Personal Ethics

In the last analysis, a researcher should not engage in any behavior that is personally offensive, even if it does not violate the governmental or professional codes of ethics. If, for example, you are adamantly opposed to using drugs, then what do you do about a possible project that will bring you into contact with people who use drugs regularly? Do you go ahead with the project and then turn your "subjects" in to the police? Do you lecture them about their evil lifestyle? Neither course of action seems very productive, and so it is best to avoid such a project entirely. Of course, we cannot always predict things that will come up, particularly in a "naturalistic" field setting. So we must have our own moral compasses ready to deal with issues that are not clearly defined by either the IRB or the relevant professional code. If you make a moral judgment that reflects your deep-seated convictions, then you must be prepared to defend it (and, perhaps, take the consequences) if it strikes others as questionable.

A student once quipped—jokingly, I hope—that it would probably be better for a researcher to be completely amoral, so that no personal qualms would ever intrude on his or her research. Questionable humor aside, I do not think that it is either possible or desirable to set aside our convictions. What makes social research so valuable is that it involves real people interacting in some way with other real people—and real people, among other things, have personal values. A truly amoral researcher could easily be replaced by a robot. I am not speaking of transient personal preferences—a woman who prefers to wear jeans might have no trouble wearing a dress if she is interviewing members of a conservative religious community. She might, however, object if she is told she must wear a full-body covering, as doing so might violate her sense of personal identity. The bottom line is that the official codes can take us only so far—legalese is not, in the long run, a substitute for our own value system, although it is a necessary and valuable starting point when we are thinking about conducting social research.

## Data Collection in the Sample Project

I began my research in earnest when I was able to take the community board's recommendation to the hospital administrator. I explained my plan to him and he gave me tentative verbal agreement, but asked me to draw up a formal statement that would spell out in full detail what I intended to do, how I intended to do it, and what I expected the end product to look like. I was, he added, to say as much as possible about the potential benefits and risks to the institution, should I be allowed to carry out my project.

The statement I drafted contained nine main points:

1. My main function at the hospital would be as a certified chaplain intern. In that capacity I would have access to all units of the hospital and could be called on by staff and patients in those units to fulfill the duties of a staff chaplain. Responding to such calls would be my first priority.

2. Once I had fulfilled any requests to act as a chaplain, I would be permitted to remain on the unit to observe its activities. The hospital administrator would respectfully request that the managers of all units cooperate with me, but ultimately the decision would be theirs—they were free to ask me to leave at any time.

3. My proposal was to be reviewed by the hospital's own IRB as well as by my university's IRB.

4. It was to be understood that selected members of the staff would be asked to sit for interviews, which would be scheduled at times and in places that would not interfere with their work.

5. Both staff and patients would be given informed consent forms apprising them of the research project; they were free to decline to participate. It was also to be made clear in the informed consent process that anything anyone chose to tell me in my capacity as a chaplain intern could not be used as part of the research; only material that people specifically indicated as "on the record" could

be used. I believe that these provisions reflect the AAA code of ethics, as well as the demands the hospital placed on me.

6. I was given access to files of internal memos (particularly those dealing with quality-of-care matters), minutes of relevant committee meetings (particularly the HEC), and materials given to new employees and volunteers at the time of their initial orientation. It was to be understood that I would not ask staff to retrieve, sort, or arrange any of this material for me. I was not to reproduce any of it without the express written permission of the relevant authority.

7. My end product was to take the form of a report to the hospital administration. It was expressly *not* to be construed as an "evaluation" of existing services, but rather as an assessment of emergent needs. It is, I believe, next to impossible to assess unmet needs without implicitly evaluating what already exists; however, reports of various accrediting agencies that periodically conduct thorough evaluations were among the materials available to me, and I was expected to rely heavily on them so that I could honestly reassure staff members that I was not observing and interviewing them for any sort of evaluation that had material consequences (e.g., denial of reaccreditation). I would not identify any of my informants, but would, to the fullest possible extent, report responses in aggregated form (e.g., "members of the nursing staff believe that . . ." not "Nurse Patty on 3-G and Dr. Jones on the trauma team believe that . . ."). If it became necessary to highlight the response of a particular individual, he or she would be identified only by his or her collective title (e.g., a nurse, a respiratory technician, a dietician, a patient, a visitor) with as little specificity as possible (e.g., not "the wife of a patient in ICU").

8. I would not be allowed to publish the report, over which the hospital would assume proprietary rights. I could, however, refer in general terms to the research for the purpose of illustrating general principles of theory and method, as I am doing in this book.

9. During the course of the project, my notes would not be stored at the hospital, but would be in a secure file in my office at the university. I was to be the sole custodian of that file; I could have one of my graduate research assistants work on the data analysis (see next chapter), but he or she would not be permitted to accompany me in "the field."

It is clear that doing research in a hospital poses a host of technical, logistical, and ethical challenges that might not obtain in a more open setting. Despite entering the situation with a recommendation from a committee with some authority, I could not simply waltz in and begin to work. I had, first of all, to prepare and present my own credentials as someone doing a "real" job at the hospital (biomedical research is a recognized and valued role; social research is, to a large extent, not so highly thought of). I then had to negotiate carefully with the administration to make sure that all aspects of informed consent, privacy, and confidentiality were protected. It turned out to be by far the most legalistically encumbered, most bureaucratic piece of research I have conducted in more than four decades as a social scientist.

I was assigned as a chaplain intern to three specific units: a surgical ward, a trauma ICU,[2] and the locked psychiatric ward. Like all members of the pastoral care staff, I was also expected to cover shifts in the emergency room and at an outpatient clinic elsewhere in the city. I decided that, rather than attempting to observe every last unit myself, I would make those units to which I was already assigned a sort of case study within the larger case study. They were, I believed, sufficiently diverse so as to provide a meaningful overview of what was going on in the hospital as a whole. I could then rely on interviews with other members of the pastoral care staff to cross-check my impressions with their views of what was going on in their own units. There seemed to be a reasonable amount of consistency across the board. Moreover, I was already a participant observer of the pastoral care department itself, which was a very important aspect of my work, since the activities of the chaplains were one of the key factors in the evolution of an ethic of care, according to the available literature. A number of the regular staff were also members of the HEC, so they were able to give me insights into that body as well.

I found that the most difficult aspect of carrying out the fieldwork was my dual role. People were sometimes puzzled at how I could split my activities as a chaplain intern from those of a researcher. I was sometimes puzzled myself. After all, a chaplain engages with people on a deeply personal level, often at times of great emotional stress. A social researcher, even one operating in a qualitative, participant mode, must of necessity be more detached, the better to grasp the big picture beyond the crisis of the moment. I was new to chaplaincy, but an old hand at research. As such, I think that I overcompensated in the former role—I was determined to do it right and was rather self-conscious about how I presented myself and how I interacted with others.[3] It was therefore a little awkward to transition back to the far more comfortable role of researcher, particularly when I was observing and/or interviewing people with whom I had already had a more intimate emotional contact—albeit one that, by the terms of my agreement with the administration, I could not legitimately use as "data."

I think that every participant observer must surmount many of the same hurdles, since this sort of research necessarily involves the assumption of one or more new roles, even as one tries to maintain a balance with one's "core" self. However, the fact that most of us are conditioned to think of a hospital as a constant drama of life and death (not necessarily always the case) adds a level of stress to the process. It is certainly possible to balance the core "self" with the role of "researcher," but it requires a good dose of introspection and reflection. I am happy that I undertook this project later in my career; I can't imagine what would have become of me had it been my first experience of fieldwork.

With regard to the technical aspects of data collection—specifically the need to be vigilant in monitoring the reliability and validity of the data themselves—I found that the most challenging problems resulted from trying to pin down the extent to which the pastoral care department and the HEC actually influenced policy, the actions of staff, and the perceptions of patients and visitors. Everyone seemed aware that this influence was part of the "big picture" at CGH, and both the chaplains and the HEC were busy and highly visible. But did that visibility necessarily translate into influence? The closer the values represented by the chaplains and the HEC were reflected in the actions of the staff even when the chaplains weren't around, the more likely it would be that a genuine, sustainable "ethic of care" was being created. If a gap existed, it would be important to find out why.

## SUGGESTIONS FOR FURTHER READING

The technical questions of reliability and validity are treated by Uwe Flick (2007), *Managing Quality in Qualitative Research* (London: Sage). Some important sources for analyses of research ethics are: D. Elliott and J. F. Stern, eds. (1997), *Research Ethics: A Reader* (Hanover, NH: University Press of New England); M. Punch (1986), *The Politics and Ethics of Fieldwork* (Beverly Hills, CA: Sage); and Carolyn Fluehr-Lobban, ed. (2003), *Ethics and the Profession of Anthropology: Dialogue for Ethically Conscious Practice, 2nd ed.* (Walnut Creek, CA: AltaMira).

## QUESTIONS FOR DISCUSSION

1. Write a formal proposal for your research, incorporating the decisions you have made to date with regard to topic, problem, literature review, research questions, and methodology. Be sure to add any relevant ethical considerations: measures to provide informed consent and to preserve privacy and confidentiality. When your proposal has been approved (either by your instructor or by your school's IRB, if necessary), you may proceed to collect your data.

2. Study the code of ethics of the AAA and at least one other social science group (e.g., the American Sociological Association). Write up a brief summary of their major points and discuss how they might be applicable to your own research.

3. See if your school's IRB recommends an online training course. (Experienced researchers are usually required to demonstrate that they keep current with regulations and practices by taking such courses every few years.) If so, go through the training just to see what issues are currently being discussed.

4. In a small discussion group, share with your classmates the personal values that you think might impact your ability (positively or negatively) to conduct social research. What can you do to enhance the positive aspects? How can you mitigate the negative ones?

5. If you were a member of the IRB at CGH, what questions might you have raised when reviewing my research proposal?

## NOTES

[1] In my role as a "chaplain intern," my conversations with patients, visitors, and staff at the hospital were "confidential." This privilege did not, however, automatically transfer to my role as a researcher.

[2] CGH has several different intensive care units; this one was designed specifically for patients who had come into the emergency room as the result of trauma (e.g., motor vehicle accident) and had had emergency surgery; they were, however, not yet sufficiently stable to be transferred to a regular room.

[3] It bears noting that I did not decide to be credentialed as a chaplain intern just as a ruse to gain entrance to the hospital to do my research. My personal values are definitely consonant with those of the pastoral care department (and of the ACPE in the broader sense). I also share the desire to see the "ethic of caring" become a real part of the hospital's operations—in that sense my applied research was designed to help CGH attain its stated goals, and hence I was not a "value neutral" scholar.

# Chapter Seven

# Analyzing Data

———◆◆◆———

After you have collected your data,
you must *analyze your findings*,
which constitutes the seventh step.

When you have completed your data collection, you will be in possession of a pile of data. But despite what conventional wisdom holds, the facts do not "speak for themselves." It is a mistake to think that numbers are the bearers of objective truth; it is up to the researcher to determine what those numbers mean. And it would be equally mistaken to think that narrative data do literally "speak." But while scattered samples of narrative set end-to-end might make for an interesting avant-garde novel, they do not tell a story that is conventionally coherent or useful for the purposes of research. It is therefore the essential task of the researcher to interpret the data—to make sense of them in some way by finding patterns, themes, or trends in the data and then explaining how and why those patterns, themes, or trends came to be.

## Data Analysis: Some General Considerations

A valid pattern is one that is shared by members of the group in their actual behavior, or is believed by members of the group to represent desirable, legitimate, or proper behavior even if they do not always practice it (in other words, their "ideal" as opposed to their actual behavior). It is very likely that unless a group is unusually homogeneous, there will be considerable diversity in the observed actual behavior of the members; there is, on the other hand, likely to be significantly more agreement with regard to the ideal behavior.[1]

Numerical data have the advantage of being analyzable by statistical means; there are many common computer programs, such as Statistical Package for the Social Sciences (SPSS) that provide convenient ways to find relevant patterns. Of course, the computer cannot do all the work—the researcher still has to input the data correctly and tell the software program what it should look for. Narrative data, on the other hand, were traditionally analyzed "manually" or (to switch the metaphor) they were "eyeballed." In other words, descriptive reports of observations and/or transcripts of interviews would be set out in print format and the researcher/analyst would look for patterns by following a process such as the following:

- Consider each statement made by someone in the community; was it made to others in everyday conversation or was it elicited by you as an interviewer?

- Consider each activity that you have observed; did it occur when you were alone with a single individual or when you were in a group setting? Was the person or group acting spontaneously or because of some prompt on your part?

In general, public statements and actions are more likely to reflect the ideal behavior of the group than are those expressed in private. Statements and activities that occur spontaneously or are volunteered by the people in the community are more likely to be elements in a shared pattern than are those somehow prompted by the researcher.

Field researchers must always be aware that things that might appear meaningful to us as outsiders might not be equally meaningful to members of the community. We have the advantage of doing a literature review and have at least a preliminary idea how our study community fits into a larger context, whereas members tend to see the world only in terms of their own experiences. The opposite is also possibly true: things that might strike us as trivial might turn out to be very important to members. As participant observers we can begin to merge these two perspectives: we gradually assimilate the "insider's" perspective without ever abandoning our comparative research-based perspective. Field researchers engage in a constant validity check by switching back and forth between the perspectives. We can do so by:

- looking for both consistencies and inconsistencies in what knowl-
edgeable members of the community tell us and probing for why
people living in the same community might disagree about matters
that seem to be important to them;

- checking what people say about behaviors and events against other
evidence, if available (e.g., news accounts, reports by others who
have conducted fieldwork in the same or similar communities),
while keeping in mind that even if what people say is factually
"wrong," their views are not to be dismissed: try to find out why
they persist in holding "erroneous" views;

- being open to "negative evidence": if a case arises that doesn't fit
our own perspective, try to find out why the discrepancy exists
(e.g., is it the result of simple diversity within the community itself?
does it reflect our lack of knowledge about the community? is it a
true anomaly that would stick out even to an experienced insider to
the community?);

- trying out alternative explanations for emergent patterns without
becoming wedded to any one explanation before all the data are in
hand.

In order to be able to conduct a systematic data analysis, whether in a
quantitative or a qualitative project, it is necessary to follow three very
important rules:

1. Keep clearly written field notes in whatever medium (computer,
   index cards, loose-leaf notebooks) you prefer or that best fit the
   demands of life in the particular field setting; if you are using
   pseudonyms or other privacy devices, be sure you remember what
   your codes refer to.

2. Devise a system of category labels that will help you file your notes
   as you collect them and that (just as important) allow you to
   retrieve them when you need them (keeping a running chronologi-
   cal narrative like a journal may be useful to you personally as a
   means of reflection, but it is nearly worthless when it comes to
   retrieving specific pieces of information). Try not to have too many
   category labels, lest you end up filing each note under a separate
   label, which will only confuse matters in the long run. As you file
   notes into categories, you will implicitly be determining which
   things go together, and in doing so you will be describing patterns.
   By the same token, do not try to work with a very small number of
   categories, as you then risk conflating statements or behaviors that

might prove to be distinct; you can always reconfigure your categories as your knowledge of the setting grows.

3. Read through your notes on a regular basis, as your research will yield far too many details for you to keep in your head for an indefinite period; such ongoing review will also prompt you to reflect on what you think you know at that point so that you can formulate questions you need to ask to fill in gaps in your knowledge.

# Using the Computer as an Aid to Data Analysis

"Eyeballing" data works well enough in discerning patterns in a relatively small-scale project; but the more data you collect, the more you will probably need to rely on computer software. There are several types of programs that you might want to explore:

- **Text retrievers** specialize in locating each occurrence of a specified word or phrase; they can also locate combinations of these items in multiple files (e.g, Orbis; ZyINDEX).

- **Textbase managers** refine the text-retrieval function and have an enhanced capacity to organize textual data (e.g., Tabletop).

- **Code-and-retrieve programs** assist researchers in dividing text into manageable sections, which can then be sorted (e.g., QUALPRO; Ethnograph).

- **Code-based theory builders** permit the development of theoretical connections between and among coded concepts, resulting in relatively high-order classifications and connections (e.g., ATLAS/ti; NUD.IST).

- **Conceptual network builders** have the capacity to design graphic networks in which variables are displayed as "nodes" that are linked to one another using arrows or lines denoting relationships (e.g., SemNet).

At the time of my sample project, I made extensive use of NUD.IST, mainly because it was being used by most of my colleagues; there was thus a good community of support—we were able to share our insights and questions. However, the choice of a program depends on your particular needs, as well as what might be available at your school, your own level of comfort with software applications, and what you can afford to buy for yourself. It is also worth keeping in mind that software development changes very rapidly. By the time you read this book, any or all of the programs mentioned in the above list might be obsolete, with new ones coming along to improve on them or even replace them completely. You will be well advised to consult up-to-date Web sites containing the most recent information about specific programs.

Computerized data analysis has several advantages:

- The software itself is a form of organized data storage, making it that much easier to retrieve material.

- Sorting and searching for text is done automatically and in far less time than would be consumed by doing so manually.

- Most programs require a careful (virtually line-by-line) examination of the data; in ordinary "eyeball" reading it is possible to skim and thus lose potentially important pieces of information.

On the other hand, a few words of caution are in order:

- There might be a steep (and time-inefficient) learning curve for new software programs.

- Although they function best as adjuncts to traditional, manual means of analysis, computer programs tempt the researcher to let them do *all* the work; you still need to give the program specific instructions about what you need it to do in the context of the particular project you are working on.

- There are many data analysis programs now available, but they are not interchangeable; it is possible to spend a lot of money buying a program (or a lot of time learning one that may be available to you at your school) only to discover that it doesn't really do what you need it to do. Do your homework about the programs before you commit yourself to one or another.

# Data Analysis: Theory

The operations discussed in the previous section will leave you with a clearly defined set of patterns and trends. But like the raw data at the beginning of the analysis process, the patterns and trends cannot and do not speak for themselves. The final (and, some would say, the most important) task of the researcher is to discern the meaning of those patterns and trends. Doing so constitutes the work of scientific *theory*. In everyday language, "theory" has come to mean nothing more than groundless opinion. "That's just a theory!" people will say when they want to dismiss someone else's ideas. In our egalitarian society, one opinion is as good as any other. But science is not a matter of opinion. Theorizing is a highly organized process that is an essential part of the overall scientific method.

Sometimes it is possible to theorize in a deductive fashion, particularly when one is working in a quantitative mode. In such cases, the potential theoretical analysis can be part of the statement that forms the research question, as the quantitative approach lends itself to projecting the kinds of patterns that one expects to emerge and that can be demonstrated statistically. Quantified data can also be analyzed using specialized software (such as SPSS) that identifies trends and patterns even in very large data sets. In qualitative research, by contrast, the perception of patterns emerges only as one immerses oneself in the data; the particular details build toward a statement of a theoretical nature, a process known as inductive reasoning.

While there are innumerable specific theories that have been developed over the decades by social scientists, they generally fall into three main categories, a familiarity with which should suffice for a preliminary research project. Two of these theoretical orientations are mainly concerned with the operations of the large-scale institutions of society; they are therefore known as "macrosocial" theories. The first of them is *functionalism*, which is concerned with the relationships among the parts of society. Functionalists tend to see those relationships as tending toward having beneficial consequences. Although sometimes a social system can exhibit dysfunctional traits, the overall tendency is for the system to reach some sort of harmonious point of equilibrium, much as the human organism (a collection of interlinked organs and organ systems) works toward a state of optimal functionality even if one or more parts is not functioning properly. For example, if one of a person's kidneys fails, he or she can still live with just one, which takes over the functions of its nonworking partner. A system that is completely out of equilibrium (like an organism overrun by metastatic cancer) can no longer function at all. Until it reaches that point, however, it can be said to be defined in terms of what it is doing to keep itself going.

The second macrosocial theory is *conflict theory*, which emphasizes a social dynamic based on competition among social groups for scarce resources. Conflict theorists are also very concerned with the operation of social, political, and economic elites and with the consequences of their ability to manipulate the allocation of goods and services to their own advantage. This is a theory that focuses on inequalities and exploitation rather than on balance and equilibrium.

The third major theoretical orientation, *symbolic interactionism*, is primarily concerned with the small-scale interpersonal dimension of social behavior and is therefore referred to as a "microsocial" approach. Symbolic interactionists look for examples of face-to-face interaction and strive to understand how groups create and use symbols to give meaning to those interactions. I chose this perspective for my CGH project. Although a hospital is, as noted earlier, an important institutional element in a large-scale social system, it is also a setting in which the abstract notion of "care" (and "efficiency," for that matter) is brought to life in the actual experiences of real people. If we want to understand what it means for a supposedly big, impersonal entity like a hospital to "care," then we have to see what happens when staff and patients interact and, in effect, negotiate meaning as they go.

"Care" cannot mean only one thing; although there may be a core of ideas that constitute "caring," the practice thereof is dependent on what people do. And what people do is dependent on whom they are doing it with and under which circumstances they do it. Observing people going about their regular activities in a natural setting and then interviewing them about what they think about what they do seemed to me a useful way to take a discussion most often couched in the literature in terms of big, broad trends and bring it down to the level of real people doing real things in real places. A microsocial approach isn't necessarily better than a macrosocial one, but given the abundance of the latter when it comes to this particular topic, it seems to be a very helpful addition.[2]

# A Concluding Note

Please note that even negative results (i.e., you did not find the pattern your deductive approach led you to expect, or you were unable to answer the question in any meaningful way after having conducted a thorough inductive inquiry) can be useful, since they establish in the literature potential dead ends or limitations on existing knowledge. We are, of course, always most happy with results that either confirm our expectations or that open up a new realm of possibilities, but do not be discouraged if you mainly establish what cannot be learned about a particular issue using a particular research technique.

# Data Analysis in the Sample Project

## Some General Findings

It was clear that CGH was making a serious effort to promote the "ethic of caring." It was, for example, running a series of slickly produced TV and print ads touting its new slogan, "Trusted for our expertise, chosen for our care." CGH has chosen to symbolize its "guiding principles" in terms of arboreal imagery: trees, leaves, and roots, which appear on logos, letterhead, and name tags, as well as most prominently in a large, stylized display in the main lobby. The hospital claims that its mission and vision can only be realized if its guiding principles take root and grow. To that end, all who work in the hospital are enjoined to be ever-mindful of the principles that are expressed by the acronyms t-r-e-e, l-e-a-f, and r-o-o-t. It is necessary to Treat others with kindness, respect, and dignity; to be Responsive to requests; to create an Environment of healing and safety; to Educate and explain. In order to make a positive impression, employees must Listen, Empathize, Act with dispatch, and Follow up. Everyone is expected to behave with Respect for everyone, regardless of status. They should Offer to help others whenever possible. There should be a sense of Organizational pride and a spirit of Teamwork.

This verbiage, which is probably a bit too cute for its own good, is enhanced by one shift in language that might be the most significant of all: patients at the hospital are now commonly referred to as "customers." Customers, after all, need to be satisfied; patients in the old days needed only to be efficiently processed.[3] In any case, staff members are given training in communication skills as part of both their initial orientation and ongoing in-service training. There is now a "pass it forward" campaign; whenever anyone in the hospital (staff, customer, or visitor) witnesses an act of special kindness, he or she presents a card (in the shape of a leaf) to the kind one. That person in turn passes the leaf to someone he or she observes performing in this approved manner. The leaf is supposed to circulate many times around the hospital.

A very important aspect of CGH's plans to create an ethic of care involves its very comprehensive bereavement program, which is based on the assumption that death is a part of life and that grief is a normal and healthy response to loss through death. The members of the bereavement care team have taken on the responsibility to provide patients' families with a dignified and respectful way to deal with the end of their loved ones' lives. Families are provided with informational resources as well as counseling services.

As previously mentioned, CGH has also instituted its own ethics committee (HEC), consisting of a multidisciplinary team of medical professionals, chaplains, social workers, professional ethicists, educators, administrators, attorneys, and laypeople representing the community at large. In one concession to the old order of things, the ethics committee is always to be chaired by a physician. Central to the work of the HEC is the principle that patients/customers are not passive recipients of treatment, but active participants in all stages of the decision-making process. (Those incapable of doing so themselves are represented by designated health care surrogates.) Customers also have the right to be informed of available resources for resolving disputes, grievances, or conflicts. The HEC, which can be contacted via a 24–hour hotline, reviews cases in order to establish broad criteria for proper behavior, although it hopes in the future to assume a proactive, rather than an after-the-fact review role.

The most visible role of the HEC at CGH is in setting guidelines regarding "advance directives" (signed statements indicating a customer's preferences regarding his or her care, particularly those at the end of life). It is increasingly common for customers to come to the hospital with advance directives already prepared (particularly if they are in life-threatening situations); the HEC will assist those who do not. The HEC also mediates in cases in which there is a discrepancy in the customer's wishes, or when there is a dispute between health care surrogates and caregivers in the absence of a valid advance care directive.

CGH has a very large pastoral care department, which it sees as integral to its vision of care. The chaplains are involved in many aspects of the hospital's work in addition to their expected spiritual ministrations. They are, for example, the primary monitors of all indigent patients, who are supposed to be given the same care enjoyed by insured customers. They also help coordinate a host of "complementary" medical practices that may be made available to customers (e.g., music therapy, visits by "therapy dogs"). They are automatically included on all treatment teams involving organ transplantation. In general the hospital recognizes the "spiritual dimension" as a vital element of modern health care.

## Analysis of Findings through the Lens of Symbolic Interactionist Theory: Pastoral Care

Based on my observations, interviews, and study of archived materials at CGH, I came to believe that there seems to be no real chance of "caring" replacing "efficiency" as the guiding virtue of hospital culture.

When the larger culture in which the medical system is a part takes stock of the quality of health care, it is almost always to the scientific and technological aspects of the system that it looks. We are certainly becoming increasingly aware of the ethical ambiguities attendant on technological expertise and of the personal costs associated with scientific advances; bioethics has become a staple topic of the popular media. But it seems highly unlikely that we would give up the technological advances (and their promise to extend and enhance the quality of life) just to achieve moral clarity and personal satisfaction.

Nevertheless, an ethic of care does seem to be playing an increased role in the way in which hospitals conceive of their mission and project an image to the public. That shift in emphasis may be due in part to an institutional concern about deflecting liability. It may also reflect a realization that a growing element in the population is looking for an ineffable "something more" than technological expertise. People who are interested in alternative or integrative medical practices cannot be easily dismissed as flaky faddists—they are expressing a very real feeling that in the face of a mighty technological behemoth it is still valuable to be recognized as individuals and to be treated with dignity and respect.

A long-standing structural problem militating against the full realization of an ethic of care is the hierarchical division of labor that marks the typical hospital. CGH, despite its commitment and serious efforts in the direction of enshrining an ethic of care as a core value within its institutional mission, is no exception. By tradition, nurses were the on-site purveyors of "care," while doctors provided "treatment" of a medical or surgical nature. Some doctors took pains to develop a pleasing "bedside manner," but when all was said and done, they were the bearers of technology and were not expected to get "too involved" with the patients as people. (Physicians in private practice have justified their increasing lack of personal involvement not by reference to the weight of scientific know-how but to the burdens of insurance and other forms of paperwork-heavy business management.)

Leaving "care" to the nurses used to be a subtle way of downplaying the importance of that ethic in the overall treatment plan. After all, nurses had extensive technical expertise—but not to the extent of the doctors. Moreover, they were mostly female. On both counts they ranked lower in the hierarchy and hence whatever was perceived as their specialty—namely "care"—could be seen as being of secondary importance.

The seeds of a true cultural shift were planted, however, as the elements in this traditional hierarchy have been redefined. For one thing, neither doctors nor nurses are as gender-specific as they once were. And in any case, the culture-at-large no longer fully accepts the old notions that only women are capable of caring and that men are incompetent at relationships. Even if there remains some truth in those old clichés, there is a gathering consensus that it needn't—shouldn't—be that way. Moreover, nurses of either gender are increasingly being asked to take on an array of technological responsibilities. At the same time, the size of nursing staffs often does not keep pace with increasing patient loads, which means that the typical nurse no longer has all that much time for traditional "caring" functions.

In the traditionally "efficient" hospital, "care" could also be parceled out to the chaplains who could easily be seen as professional hand-holders with even fewer technical responsibilities than nurses to divert them from their ministrations. But since chaplains were often outsiders with responsibilities to congregations of their own elsewhere in the community, they had relatively little interaction with the other players in the world of the hospital. While treated with respect, they did not, as a group, figure very highly in the overall status system. Even in those hospitals that support a resident pastoral care department, it has been easy to proceed with the traditional division of labor and to relegate the chaplains to the most obviously "spiritual" elements of care.

At CGH the role of the pastoral care department has been greatly expanded due to circumstances that are not necessarily found in all hospitals. First, there is the fact that the CGH pastoral care department hosts a large C.P.E. program, which means that at any given time there are far more in-house chaplains of one sort or another available to participate in on-site activities. Second, there is the fact that the current director of pastoral care has been unusually assertive in making his staff, residents, and interns available for duties that do not, on the face of it, seem to be "spiritual" in nature. For example, chaplains on duty in the Emergency Room are often involved in helping the police and other authorities establish the identities of trauma victims who are brought in without IDs. They are also the ones who call to notify relatives that a loved one has been brought into the ER, and they meet those relatives when they arrive at the hospital and escort them through the maze of the ER. The chaplains are also responsible for monitoring the expenses incurred by indigent patients. Both of these functions can be said to represent "caring" in a very general sense, but in ways hardly envisioned by the prayer-saying, spiritual-counseling chaplains of previous times. The CGH pastoral care department has therefore embraced the most expansive definitions of the role of the hospital chaplaincy; it must, however, be kept in mind that both in the scholarly literature and in actual practice, there is still a strong body of more conservative opinion that resists the use of chaplains and associated pastoral personnel in any but the most clearly demarcated "spiritual" domains.

A third factor at play at CGH is the fact that pastoral care is explicitly nondenominational; all the chaplains (whether staff, resident, pool, intern) are encouraged to be faithful to their own traditions but to avoid overtly partisan denominationalism in their ministry. To be sure, some patients actually prefer chaplains from their own church—there is undeniably a certain comfort to be had from someone who "speaks your own language," especially when you are in a weakened condition. But many more do not. Indeed, it seemed (on the basis of my experience, at least) that a large number of people who would reject the services of a chaplain for fear of his or her sectarian bias are more than happy to discuss their concerns with someone who has made it clear that he or she has no such agenda.

One of the trends in contemporary religion in modern society, particularly in the United States, is the move away from affiliation with formal religious bodies and toward a more general "spiritual" orientation. The forces that have always led people to religion (e.g., the need to be able to explain "the big picture," the need to feel some sense of control in an otherwise chaotic and dangerous cosmos) remain strong, but the nature of our society makes commitment to one particular church seem a bit quaint and limiting. The "spiritualization" of pastoral care at CGH (as opposed to an older sectarian/denominational approach to religiosity) is thus a particularly clearly realized factor in its appropriation of the central role as care agent at the hospital.

Even at CGH, however, the fact that there is a designated "care" office means that other staff members do not have to take an active part in the delivery of care. I do not mean this statement to be as harsh as it may sound. I am convinced that almost everyone at the hospital is actively engaged in "caring *for*" patients (and even visitors). Caring *for* someone means carrying out actions in service to others. It goes almost without saying that doctors, nurses, and all other staffers are well trained, highly skilled, and carry out their assigned duties in the appropriate manner. What often seems to be lacking, however, is the sense of "caring *about*" people.

Nurses are increasingly becoming like doctors to the extent that they are now more guarded about becoming "too involved" with the patients—again, partly because of liability concerns, partly because they are simply carrying overwhelming caseloads. But I do believe that patients (and visitors) can tell the difference. They appreciate the level of expertise involved in the ways the staff cares *for* them, but they often express regret that they are not being seen or heard or otherwise paid attention to as people. Not that much has changed since the time when patients were literally made to feel like "the gall stones in 610."

It was pretty clear to me, as well as to patients and visitors, when staff members stepped out of the box and acted in ways that indicated that they really did care *about* them. And it was just as clear that such expressions of concern were deeply appreciated. I cannot, of course, document the impression that patients who feel cared *about* in addition to being cared *for* have better treatment outcomes, but I am convinced that any hospital that is serious about its ethic of care needs to inculcate that value throughout the staff, and not segregate it as the exclusive preserve of the pastoral care department, no matter how much involved the chaplains may be beyond the purely "spiritual" realm.

The highly personal, particularistic nature of my involvement with the hospital reinforces my predilection for a "symbolic interactionist" approach to the interpretation of what I learned. This form of social theory is particularly concerned with the meanings people give to things they do and experience; in looking at the relationship between individual perceptions and the organization of society, it emphasizes the way people create, negotiate, and change social meanings as they interact with each other. The first major premise of symbolic interactionism is that the objects, events, individuals, groups, and structures we encounter do not have an inherent or unvarying meaning. It is therefore important to know how people define those elements in order to understand how they will react to them.

An example of the above is my observance of the ICU nurses, following standard procedure, entered a certain patient on the tracking chart as "John Doe" because he had not been officially identified when he was brought into the ER; his name had not been changed in the system by the time he was transferred to ICU; in order to track the patient efficiently, the "John Doe" would have to follow him until it was officially changed. The fact that his identity remained a John Doe did not affect his level of care by the hospital staff. Nevertheless, to the family, the fact that the Doe name was up on the board for all to see was a sign not of efficiency but of disrespect, a denial of the personhood of their injured relative. The family had no quarrel with the technical expertise of the ICU staff—for them, it was not an issue of their relative being cared *for*. But they did feel that no one cared *about* him because he was being referred to in a way that would be considered insulting and demeaning anywhere outside the hospital.

The second major premise of the theory is that meanings come from social interactions. The ICU staff, like everyone else who regularly works in the hospital, knows perfectly well what a "Doe name" signifies and why it is used. No one at the hospital thought it worthwhile to interact with the family in a way that would carefully explain the delay in posting the patient's real name. "It's procedure," the family was told in a brisk, almost dismissive way. True enough, but in the absence of a real interaction, the "procedure" remained meaningless, and hence threatening.

Examples of such symbolic miscommunication abound. A patient in the surgical unit was constantly wandering around the floor despite limitations on her mobility. Her behavior was seen by the nurses as a sign that she was restless and somewhat disoriented. She saw her own behavior, rather, as a manifestation of her anxiety about her son, who was away at war in Iraq. No one except the chaplain (a regular staff chaplain) had bothered to ask what stresses and anxieties she had brought to the hospital with her. It did not occur to the medical and nursing staff that she had any concerns beyond the condition that required surgery.

One seriously injured man in the ER was wearing a wedding ring; as his hand was badly swollen, a nurse attempted (with rather alarming vigor) to take it off. The man whispered to me that he wanted to keep the ring—it was a way of keeping his late wife close to him during his ordeal. The nurse was thinking of the ring in purely pragmatic terms—it was a hindrance to proper treatment. The gentleman, however, saw it as a token of great sentimental value. But it would be wrong to dichotomize such situations and assume that the two sides hold absolutely different views (each of them set in concrete) and simply need to explain their ideas more clearly. The fact is that meanings shift (they are "negotiated," to use the theoretical jargon) and that sometimes multiple meanings may be held.

The third premise of the theory, then, is that when multiple meanings are in play, a constant process of interpretation must be carried out so that people know how to respond in the context of a given situation. When I first met a Native American family in the ER, for example, their rather distant, uncooperative manner could be interpreted in any of several ways. They could have been in shock over the severity of the auto accident that had claimed the life of one man, whose seriously injured son was now being treated; they might not have been able to speak English very well; they were hiding something (perhaps the driver had been intoxicated at the time of the crash?). I chose to go with another interpretation, one that reflected my own anthropological leanings (and the fact is that in that case I had been specifically summoned *because* I am an anthropologist): that their behavior had something to do with what their matrilineal cultural traditions taught them to consider about the proper way to show respect to their absent grandmother, for once the lady finally appeared, their interactions became much easier—they had been in a state of suspended animation, waiting for her lead. Actually, their behavior may have been the result of more than one of these motives, but I had to make an interpretation that allowed me to interact with them in what I thought would be the most mutually beneficial manner.

On the whole, interactionists believe that people exercise freedom of choice when deciding how to act and how to react to others' actions. People are, of course, highly influenced by forces beyond their control, such as the physical or mental condition that brought them to the hospital in the first place. Someone who is having seizures is not acting of his or her own volition by thrashing around or falling to the floor. And the observer would be mistaken in attributing such actions to anything other than a medical condition in need of immediate attention. But beyond such obvious constraints, a great deal of what we say and do comes from what we choose to say and do.

Even people who are weak, in pain, or otherwise compromised in their regular social capacities can manage to convey their point of view. For example, although it was very difficult for one young man (a robust athlete who was paralyzed after an accident) to move himself, he forced himself to turn over and present his back to me as a way of shutting off any possible interaction. He clearly intended to send me a message, and he did so, even though it took a great deal of physical effort. He was clearly not ready to deal with what he perceived as an irreparable loss, at least not with an older man whom he equated with his judgmental father and coach. He readily opened up to a female chaplain. A man at the community clinic, although blind and hence "disabled" in conventional terms, very definitely used the vehement tapping of his cane as a way to convey his annoyance at being treated disrespectfully by the staff in the waiting room.

As an anthropologist I have often been struck by the way people have latched onto the culture concept in ways that make it seem very much like an immutable behavioral constraint, like a physical disability. It is often assumed that only manifestly exotic people have culture (which is probably why I was summoned when the Native American clan showed up in the ER) so that we, who are obviously "normal" have to go out of our way to "understand" them. The subtext of this attitude is that "the others" are so deeply mired in the coils of their traditional culture that they can never be anything but what that culture dictates. In fact, the interactionist perspective is based on the contrary assumption—that everyone has a range of options for action, some (but by no means all) of them reflecting the constraints of traditional culture.

It is important to remember, therefore, that interactions require at least two players. Hospital staff cannot be truly caring if all they do is monitor the symbolic gambits of the patients and visitors and fail to be fully cognizant of their own. We all need to be more self-aware about the messages we send through body language, gesture, or tone of voice. For example, we chaplain interns were always told never to sit on a patient's bed, not only because it could cause them to have an uncomfortable or even painful shift in weight, but because it could seem like a threatening invasion of what little remains of their private space. But most of us admitted to feeling awkward standing up and looming over a prone patient—the position of authority assumed without question by doctors and nurses. So if possible we tried to bring a chair to the bedside so that we would be on eye-level with the patient. If that was not possible (and in some of the smaller shared rooms there was almost no space in which to move a chair) we squatted at the bedside (kneeling might convey a message of excessive piety that might not have been appropriate in all situations). One of my colleagues once reported that he was squatting beside a frail patient who said to him, "You look awfully uncomfortable down there. Why don't you just sit on the bed?" Indeed, there are rules—and then there are social imperatives.

In the CGH context, we might all do well to be a bit more conscious of when our "good show" behavior comes off all too obviously *as* "show." This point relates to the fundamental principle of pastoral counseling as I came to understand it through the C.P.E. course: that we minister to others first by being attentive to who they are and what they are trying to convey to us (as often as not through the symbolic language of gesture and tone as by straightforward verbalization) and second by being attentive to ourselves, the messages we are sending out, and the sources (both positive and negative) of our self-expression. Once again, the lesson is clear: you cannot minister to the "whole person" in the other unless you are aware of and in touch with the "whole person" in yourself.

Interactionists contend that social life consists of "joint action," or what people do together. Joint action is often routine and repetitive in that people have a more or less clear understanding of how they need to behave and how others will react to their behavior. They draw on a set of shared and ready-made meanings, often encapsulated in recognizable social roles. When a patient lying in a hospital bed sees a nurse approach with a needle, he or she knows pretty much what to expect, and while the act may be uncomfortable or even painful, it would not be considered strange. The patient has learned to recognize the nurses by the way they dress, the way they talk, and so forth. On the other hand, if the person brandishing the syringe was dressed in a Halloween Frankenstein costume and smelled of liquor, then the patient would have ample reason to be alarmed; the symbolic language conveying the message "it's all right" had been altered and rendered problematic. So although we know that meanings can and do shift and that multiple meanings are possible, ordinary social life is made possible because we can usually ignore those mixed messages and proceed as if we knew what to expect.

One of the problems involved of pastoral care is that the role relationships are not nearly as clearly understood as are the relationships of doctors or nurses with patients. Since the chaplain enters a patient's room dressed in civilian clothes with only a badge as a mark of special status (and a patient lying in bed is not always in a position to read the badge), patients can be forgiven for not knowing exactly how to respond. Because of the nondenominational status of the hospital chaplain, we were not permitted to wear anything that might symbolize our own religious affiliations outside the hospital. For this reason, chaplains were asked to dress in formal business attire (i.e., not "business casual"). It might not always be clear who the chaplain is in terms of a readily defined hospital role (and, to be honest, a fair number of people were unfamiliar with the very title "Chaplain"), but at least it's clear that he or she is not just some casual visitor off the street.[4]

Joint action, moreover, is linked to a complex network of actions that provide layers of context for it. For example, the nurse carrying the needle is dependent on the hospital pharmacy supplying the correct medication, on the pharmaceutical manufacturer for producing the drug, on the shipping company or postal service for getting the product from the manufacturer to the hospital, and so forth. In the same way, it must be remembered that the apparently simple action of a chaplain entering a room to offer pastoral care is dependent on that person's knowledge of counseling, degree attainment, or achievement of some other form of ordination or certification, and on certification by the hospital to work in the pastoral care department. That same simple act also carries cultural baggage, which is the third dimension of joint action. For example, there is the church or faith tradition to which the chaplain belongs (and represents, if only implicitly) and the theology of ministry that led him or her to this career choice. On the other side, there are the imponderable reactions of the patient (what has been the patient's prior experience with religious professionals?)

In sum, joint acts are the results of an ongoing process of construction. In other words, they are subject to unforeseen contingencies and changes. When we participate in joint action—even the most apparently routine ones—we are apt to be surprised (or to cause surprise), misunderstood (or to cause misunderstanding), or to become involved in unintended conflict.

Perhaps the most important lesson I learned about the institutionalization of an ethic of care in a modern hospital is that those in a position of authority labor under the false impression that they can mandate it and provide specific, step-by-step training for it in the same way that they can offer orientations about fire safety or how to make a note on a patient's chart. The great strength of pastoral care, at least as it is practiced at CGH, is that it is radically open to contingency and to the perception that not every situation is cut-and-dried and has an immediate and clearly defined solution. That perspective, however, is not widely shared, even among those elements in the system most committed to providing a caring atmosphere. Until that philosophy is inculcated across the board among those who function within the orbit of the hospital, the hospital will remain a top-notch place in which to be cared *for*, but not one in which patient, visitor, and staff member alike can feel truly cared *about*.

## Analysis of Findings: The HEC

HECs were set up to deal primarily with ethical questions affecting individuals (whether patients or staff); they also have been obliged to consider additional issues affecting the institution, such as corporate structure, as well as the society to which the institution is attached. At CGH, there is a dawning realization that decisions traditionally thought of as financial, administrative, or organizational have important ethical implications. The area of budgetary planning and resource allocation, for example, is no longer understood simply as the preserve of the accountants. When budgetary allocations begin to affect the level, extent, and quality of care, then making "triage" decisions becomes a very explicitly ethical matter. Hospitals have traditionally adopted a "silo effect"—the tendency to want to separate individual ethical questions from institutional ones. But the HEC at CGH is implicitly advocating for a more integrated model; because the nature of the organization shapes the kind of clinical cases that are of concern in a hospital.

Moreover, ethics committee members are affected by what is going on in the society around them and, at the very least, they can use issues currently under debate as "teachable moments" for the educational component of their charge. But there is also growing sentiment that they can and should insert themselves more directly into the debate, although questions remain about the wisdom of doing so. For example, should committees be involved in the public policy (as opposed to strictly institutional policy) process by attempting to influence legislation or by persuading voters about legislative initiatives? Should they take public positions about hot-button health care issues? Some ethics committees have, in fact, delegated members to testify at state legislative hearings, and others have filed briefs in court cases. While individual members of the committee may feel strongly about taking a public stand, there is a powerful countervailing force at work, and once again it reflects expediency rather than philosophy. That is, does the committee risk alienating important segments of a community divided on an issue if it takes a stand on one side or the other? If it actively pursues a lobbying role, does the committee jeopardize the institution's tax-exempt status (if it is a charitable organization) or its future budgetary status (if, like CGH, it is a public institution)? Since HECs are on the frontlines of many important ethical controversies, it would be a shame if they let prudence stand in the way of their ability to share their expertise beyond their institutional walls. But, as an ethics committee member told me only somewhat in jest, the "cult of covering-your-ass" is probably even more pervasive in large bureaucracies like hospitals than is the more widely discussed "cult of efficiency."

The importance of these institutional and social issues notwithstanding, the core of the HEC's activities at CGH remains in consult/case review. In the nearly two decades that HECs have been common features of the institutional landscape, a basic format for the consult has emerged; it is followed with but minor variations in most hospitals, including CGH. The case review template addresses the following questions:

- What is the relevant medical information?
- Is the patient capable of making medical decisions?
- If not, who is the appropriate decision maker?
- How does the surrogate justify his or her decision?
- Have all the appropriate parties met and discussed the case?

- Are there any important legal constraints?
- What conclusions can be drawn from all the above information?
- What course of action can be recommended?

My observations of the HEC at CGH, interviews with its members, and analysis of its archived reports/minutes can be summarized as follows:

- **Organization**. The committee has 30 designated members, of whom 20 are regular participants (near the high end as compared with national averages). The committee is chaired by a physician as mandated in the committee's charter; the physicians as a group threatened to boycott the HEC if anyone but a physician chaired it.[5] A variety of medical specialties are represented, most notably surgical services and internal medicine, followed rather distantly by social services (including pastoral care). Emergency services and intensive care were both underrepresented. It seems to be taken for granted that people who work in those units are too busy to undertake committee work, but one has to wonder how assiduously they were courted, given the centrality of those services to most ethical issues. As for nonclinical personnel, the committee shows heavy representation by administrative staff and personnel from the legal counsel's office. There was also a professional ethicist who works with the committee, although she functions mainly as a "consult specialist" rather than as a regular member. Except for the professional ethicist and the pastoral care people (who typically take courses in ethics as part of their professional training), most members of the committee do not have specific training in ethics, but rather are chosen on the basis of their personal experience in the medical field. Once on the committee, however, many of them choose (but are not required) to take continuing education workshops, if not full courses, in bioethics.

- **Operations**. There are regular quarterly meetings of the committee, although there might be meetings in between if the case review volume warrants. Perhaps because CGH is a major teaching institution, its HEC seems to be particularly outspoken on social issues. The committee regularly sponsors presentations and other types of informal (i.e., noncoursework) educational programs for hospital staff; these programs are also open to interested members of the public. The committee functions at the low end of the institution's budgetary scale; its administrative and clerical duties (e.g., preparing and disseminating minutes, organizing programs, taking care of correspondence) are done on a volunteer basis by the members with minimal assistance from administrative staff. There is, however, a small supplemental budget for buying books and other educational resources, which are housed in the medical library. There is little or no official communication between the HEC at CGH and the analogous committees at the other large hospitals in the metropolitan area, even though the three hospitals collectively represent by far the largest patient population in the service area and might well benefit from interinstitutional coordination (e.g., educational programs).

- **Policy development**. At CGH, the ethics committee has not yet had a major impact beyond specific case decisions, but because its pastoral care department is unusually aggressive in inserting its staff chaplains in all manner of hospital operations, the "caring" segment can be said to be well represented in policy-making circles. The HEC at CGH has developed a statement of patient rights that is prominently posted and is given to all new admissions, although it is doubtful that most patients are aware of its existence.

- **Consults**. The main work of the committee is its consults, with between 12 and 15 per calendar year—markedly above the reported national average. The vast majority of requests for consults came from professional staff and almost all of them dealt with end-of-life issues. At CGH there were also a few cases in which patients who, unbeknownst to EMTs, had do-not-resuscitate (DNR) orders, and so were resuscitated in the ambulance. In the technical sense, such a violation of a DNR order in our state can lead to prosecution for battery. But in the case reported, the EMTs and the hospital were able to take shelter behind a good faith/Good Samaritan provision in the law. There have also been some cases involving the proper treatment of patients whose religious views preclude certain types of otherwise routine medical or surgical procedures (e.g., Jehovah's Witnesses who will not accept blood transfusions). I expected to find cases at CGH having to do with the implications of providing care for indigent patients, but no such cases materialized while I was conducting my research. (I suspect this to be a matter of short-term, random chance rather than a real trend for the long term.)

- **Evaluation**. The committee did not have a defined process for self-evaluation, and it was resistant to the idea of hiring an outsider to do such an evaluation. (I had to work diligently to convince some members that I was not an undercover evaluator.) The committee is, however, reviewed—albeit in a somewhat cursory fashion—in the course of JCAHO surveys.

The question remains: has the ubiquity of HECs led to a more noticeably caring atmosphere in modern hospitals? CGH's new advertising motto proclaims: "Trusted for our expertise; chosen for our care." Can such a boast be justified? I cannot answer the question on a national basis, but such a shift is definitely underway, albeit in a very preliminary fashion. Even if it represents only a fear of litigation, it is important to note that such fear has led the hospital to embrace practices, policies, and interpersonal relationships that are distinctively different from those that characterized them in the past. To analyze this process more clearly, we might make use of the notion of corporate culture.

The concept of corporate culture has not always been well regarded by anthropologists, but some of its main principles can be refracted through the lens of symbolic interactionist theory to make them more palatable. For our purposes, we can say that corporate culture comprises the attitudes, values, beliefs, norms, and customs of an organization. It relies on the support of an organizational structure (represented by the familiar corporate flowchart) but, like culture in general, transcends the social structure. We can characterize corporate culture as the result of a dynamic interplay among several key factors:

- the **paradigm** (the organization's mission and values);
- the **control system** (the processes in place to monitor what is going on);
- **organizational structures** (reporting lines, hierarchies, the flow of "work" through the system);
- **power structures** (who makes the decisions, how widely the power is spread, the source of the power);
- **symbols** (logos and letterheads most obviously, but also such things as parking spaces and executive washrooms);
- **rituals** and **routines** (management meetings, board reports, operating practices);
- **stories** and **myths** (narratives about people and events that are passed along—usually informally—that convey a message about what is valued within the organization).

Hospitals are examples of institutions exhibiting what the literature calls "strong culture." That is, they are staffed by people who are firmly aligned with organizational values, specifically the values that constitute the prevailing "cult of efficiency," which is inculcated in staff members from the time they enter medical, nursing, therapist, or other health care professional training (with the exception of chaplaincy). "Strong" corporate cultures are prone to "groupthink," a situation in which people, even if they have different ideas, do not challenge organizational thinking. Members who deviate from the corporate line are marginalized because their unorthodox views disturb the central culture. As in any culture, there is a tendency toward ethnocentrism—the view that "our" way of doing things is the best and that everything else is at best an annoyance and at worst a mortal threat. The question thus arises: how does a "strong" corporate culture engage in an institutional paradigm shift involving that very culture?

There are five characteristics of a culture that must be assessed if we are to come up with an overall appreciation for its openness to change:

1. **Power distance** is the degree to which there is an expected difference in power. Hospitals are by tradition hierarchical, centralized, and authoritarian rather than egalitarian in their organization, a factor that suggests that change, if it comes, must emanate from the top. To be sure, the "top" is itself shifting; while doctors are still the most prestigious members of the organization, hospitals are in effect run by businesspeople who control the corporate structures of which the hospitals are a part; such people also dominate hospitals' community boards of directors. Nevertheless, hospitals are "role cultures," ones in which people have clearly delegated authorities within a highly defined structure; power derives from a person's position and little scope exists for the exercise of initiative outside recognized role boundaries. On the other hand, since the current situation (even if it is mainly the result of a fear of litigation) requires the development of attitudes and behaviors not covered by the traditional role set, there is clearly room for change.

2. **Uncertainty avoidance** is the extent to which risk is embraced. In our age of medical litigation, no hospital can afford much exposure to risk, so that for any change to be embraced it must be presented as minimizing risk to the fullest possible extent. Such a corporation has a "work hard/play hard culture," one in which few risks are taken but with rapid feedback (monetary, or more intangibly, in terms of prestige) for those that are ventured. They suggest that such cultures are typical of large organizations that strive for "high-quality customer service," which certainly describes a hospital.

3. **Social orientation** is the degree to which people think either individualistically or collectively. In hospitals, individual initiative is prized only at the top levels of the hierarchy—we often hear praise for "pioneering surgeons" who try bold new procedures, but we

rarely, if ever, see the "maverick nurse" as an object of admiration (except on TV hospital melodramas), as nurses are expected to be subordinate team players, not leaders. This premise once again argues for innovation as emanating from those in the hierarchy who are culturally sanctioned as innovators. We assume that this means that they never truly *are* innovators, since they have too much invested in the status quo. But on the other hand, failure to embrace "caring" has some very negative consequences for the institution (in terms of both public relations and legal entanglements), and so those at the top might well embrace change simply in an effort to maintain their relative position within the hierarchy.

4. **Value orientation** is categorized in the literature of corporate culture in rather unfortunately sexist terms: it is either "masculine" (stressing competitiveness, assertiveness, ambition, the accumulation of wealth and material possessions) or "feminine" (stressing cooperation, nurturance, a tendency to be concerned about people rather than abstractions). In the stereotype, "efficiency" is a "masculine" value while "caring" is a "feminine" one. In order for a "masculine" corporate culture to embrace a "feminine" value like caring, it must be shown to have a definite payoff and not simply be good for its own sake.

5. **Time orientation** is the degree to which a culture emphasizes the past, the present, or the future in its self-image. Hospitals, like most modern corporations, are decidedly future-oriented, at least to judge by the proliferation of their "mission statements" and "projections" and "target goals." For example, CGH proudly proclaims its "vision" of being "at the forefront of clinical services, medical research and education. With our physicians and university partners we will create, teach and deliver tomorrow's breakthroughs in medical science." In that context, "caring" would seem to be a rather old-fashioned virtue, but only as long as it is tied to the time-consuming "hand-holding" image of the chaplains of yesteryear. Is there a way to integrate "caring" into the cutting-edge vision of the future?

This latter ambiguity is further illuminated if we see corporate culture as existing on three interrelated, but clearly distinct cognitive levels (i.e., as it can come to be known by the outsider). At the most cursory level, the culture is defined by things that can be seen, felt, and heard by the uninitiated observer (e.g., facilities, furnishings, awards on display, the way personnel dress and interact with each other). The second level is a matter of the culture as described by participants themselves. It is embodied in company slogans, mission and vision statements, and operational policies. This level of culture is best studied through interviews or questionnaires. The third level is one at which the tacit assumptions of the culture are embedded. These elements are not easily perceived through casual observation and are not even necessarily consciously recognized by the participants. They form a body of unspoken rules that may take on the characteristics of tabooed speech or behavior—the sort of things no one will tell you about, but of which you become aware when you inadvertently violate one of the rules. It is usually at this level that change in corporate culture will be halted, since that which is unspoken is virtually impossible to address, let alone challenge. But it is possible to understand what is going on at this level by means of careful, in-depth interviews and extended participant observation, exactly the sort of research that could be carried out by an anthropologist.

The physicians' threats notwithstanding, the plain fact is that a hospital probably cannot function without its HEC and still maintain its accreditation. Moreover, an HEC operates in such a way as to subtly, but decisively shift traditional relationships and balances of power. HECs are therefore a vehicle whereby the supposedly ingrained abuses of the old cult of efficiency are modified. As long as the hospital must traffic in the sort of services that can only be provided by a small group of initiates who retain tight control over access to training in that expertise, it must surely remain an authoritarian institution in which depersonalization is the norm. But the model of consensus decision making in service to individual rights and personal responsibilities is one that represents a clear evolution in the way the hospital does business.

## SUGGESTIONS FOR FURTHER READING

Graham R. Gibbs (2007), *Analyzing Qualitative Data* (London: Sage) provides an excellent, detailed overview of the processes and practices of data analysis.

Standard works that provide an overview of social theory include George Ritzer (2008), *Classic Sociological Theory, 5th ed.* (New York: McGraw-Hill) and R. Jon McGee and Richard L. Warms (2004), *Anthropological Theory: An Introductory History, 3rd ed.* (Boston: McGraw-Hill); the former focuses on the discipline of sociology, while the latter deals primarily with cultural anthropology.

A good introduction to symbolic interactionist theory is provided by Kent L. Sandstrom, Daniel D. Martin, and Gary Alan Fine (2003), *Symbols, Selves, and Social Reality: A Symbolic Interactionist Approach to Social Psychology and Sociology* (Los Angeles: Roxbury Press). For a view on the application of this perspective to the study of the institution of medicine, see Kathy Charmaz and Virginia Olesen (2003), "Medical Institutions" (pp. 637–656) in *Handbook of Symbolic Interactionism*, edited by Larry T. Reynolds and Nancy J. Herman-Kinney (Walnut Creek, CA: AltaMira).

An anthropological analysis of the role of the hospital chaplain is provided by Frances Norwood (2006), "The Ambivalent Chaplain: Negotiating Structural and Ideological Differences on the Margins of Modern-Day Hospital Medicine," *Medical Anthropology* 25(1):1–19.

Issues in hospital ethics in general and the function of HECs in particular are treated by Judith Andre (1997), "Goals of Ethics Consultation: Toward Clarity, Utility, and Fidelity," *Journal of Clinical Ethics* 8(2):193–198; James F. Drane (1994), *Clinical Bioethics* (Kansas City MO: Sheed and Ward); Mary Beth Foglia and Robert A. Pearlman (2006), "Integrating Clinical and Organizational Ethics," *Health Progress* 87(2):31–35; Jack Freer (2006), *How to Perform an Ethics Consult* (Buffalo, NY: Center for Clinical Ethics and Humanities in Health Care); Elizabeth Heitman and Ruth Ellen Bulger (1998), "The Healthcare Ethics Committee in the Structural Transformation of Health Care: Administrative and Organizational Ethics in Changing Times," *Healthcare Ethics Committee Forum* 10(2):152–176; Kevin Murphy (2006), "A 'Next Generation' Ethics Committee," *Health Progress* 87(2):26–30; Robert Lyman Porter (1996), "From Clinical Ethics to Organizational Ethics: The Second Stage of the Evolution of Bioethics," *Bioethics Forum* 12(2):3–12; Judith Wilson Ross, Corinne Bayley, Vicki Michel, and Deborah Pugh, eds. (1986), *Ethics Committees: The Next Generation* (Chicago: American Hospital Association).

Perspectives on corporate culture are provided by Terrence E. Deal and Allan A. Kennedy (1982), *Corporate Cultures: The Rites and Rituals of Corporate Life* (Harmondsworth: Penguin); Irving L. Janis (1983), *Groupthink: Psychological Studies of Policy Decisions and Fiascoes, 2nd ed.* (Boston: Houghton Mifflin); Martin Parker (2000), *Organizational Culture and Identity* (London: Sage); Edgar H. Schein (2004), *Organizational Culture and Leadership, 3rd ed.* (San Francisco: Jossey-Bass).

## QUESTIONS FOR DISCUSSION

1. Select a method for finding patterns in the data you have collected (e.g., manual use of statistics, computer-assisted statistical analysis, manual narrative analysis, computer-assisted narrative analysis). Make sure that your field notes are organized to allow you to retrieve your data in a way that will make your analytical method most efficient. Proceed to analyzing your data.

2. Try applying each of the three theoretical orientations as you explore the meaning of the patterns you have found. Which one seems to work best? Explain why.

## NOTES

[1] I realize that putting the matter in these terms makes it sound like I am accusing most people of being hypocrites. I would rather say that real life imposes numerous challenges that make it difficult to live up to one's ideals. Living culture is always a matter of negotiation and compromise. That does not make the ideal any less relevant; there is a big difference between a community that cannot consistently live up to its ideals and a community that has amorally given up on having ideals at all—and most people fit well into the former category.

[2] In the interest of full disclosure, I should note that I tend to use an interactionist perspective in most of my research. I like the emphasis on "playing the game" (as distinct from "understanding the rule book") that this perspective affords. I therefore tend to gravitate toward research problems that lend themselves to a microsocial view.

[3] The use of the term "customers" is not yet universally accepted. I will therefore continue to use the more common, familiar term, "patients," except when referring specifically to CGH's official policy statements.

[4] A controversy arose at the time of my study, and has gathered some momentum in the years since: men's neckties are a potential source of infection since, unlike other items of clothing, they are laundered only infrequently. So some of the chaplains argued for omitting the tie despite the rule of "business attire." Their point was not adopted at the time, but the neckties-are-icky faction has become more vocal and influential over the years.

[5] It is not clear whether they could have done so without jeopardizing the hospital's accreditation, but they nonetheless got their point across.

# Chapter Eight

# **Sharing Results**

---

## At the eighth step you
## *share your results*
## in some appropriate fashion.

The point of doing scientific research is to become part of the ongoing discourse—the never-ending round of questions and responses that makes it possible to understand the world around us. Research results that you keep locked up in your own file cabinet are essentially worthless. Sometimes ethical constraints preclude the sharing of research because they might harm your informants or somehow inflame public opinion, but for the most part it is a good thing to get the word out to one's scientific peers and even to audiences beyond academe. At first, your audience may be no larger than your instructor or other students in your class. But at some point you may be ready to publish your results, either in the form of a conference paper, a journal article, or a posting on a suitable Web site. You may also want to contribute your findings to a social agency interested in furthering goals, using your findings to help their cause.

## **Representing Your Data: The Traditional Form**

For most of the history of scientific research, the appropriate product for sharing results was the scholarly manuscript, which might be a book-length *monograph* (an in-depth treatment of a single subject) or textbook;

it might also have been an article published in a peer-reviewed journal, a chapter in an edited volume, or a paper presented at a professional conference. Although there are many other options available to the modern researcher, we will consider this traditional scholarly form first, given its prominence in the history of scientific research.

Scientific writing of either article/chapter/paper or book length typically includes several key elements set out in a conventional order.

- A **title** is a description of the contents; it should not be too cute or clever or literary.

- An **abstract** is a brief (100–200 words) overview of the research, featuring the most important findings. It includes a brief description of the methods by which data were collected and analyzed. It closes with a statement of the implications of the major findings. There is little or no explanation or illustrative detail in the abstract, which, in a book-length work, might be replaced by a **preface** of relatively greater length and involving a little more detail.

- An **introduction** orients the audience to the study. It includes a statement explaining (and, if need be, justifying) the main research questions and an overview of the key issues to be discussed.

- A **literature review** entails a critical examination of the relevant published materials, with attention to the development of the author's own theoretical orientation.

- A **methodological review** explains (and perhaps justifies) research procedures in detail.

- A report of **findings** or **results** should be a clear linkage between what has been discovered and the research question(s)/hypotheses that the researcher began with and issues that were prominent in the literature review.

- A **concluding discussion** summarizes the main findings and situates this particular piece of research into some larger body of literature. Directions for future research may also be appropriate in this section (either research that the author intends to do him or herself or that he or she is recommending to the scientific community at large).

- **References, notes,** and **appendices** are explanatory materials supplemental to the main body of the text. Notes may be part of the text, placed at the foot of the page, or grouped at the end of the chapter or of the entire book. Notes must never convey substantive information that should be in the text. References are to all cited material (although there may be a separate section of "works not cited but consulted by the author") and must follow the standard form authorized by the journal or publisher. Appended materials might include charts or tables, copies of original documents, photos, or any other matter that supports the main elements of the text.

In addition to conforming to this fairly rigid format, a piece of traditional scientific writing was expected to be written in an impersonal manner (older standards banned the use of the pronoun "I," although that prohibition has been relaxed in recent years) without rhetorical flourishes. Traditional academic writing often struck those unfamiliar with its conventions as being "dry" or "dull" because it so studiously avoided colorful language and personal means of expression. Except to the initiate, it was often difficult to read or listen to; some critics have unkindly suggested that this forbidding style was deliberately cultivated to maintain academic science as a carefully regarded preserve of the elite. I personally doubt that there was ever a conscious, let alone a sinister plot to achieve that goal. Rather, I suspect that after four years of college, at least four more of graduate school, and then years of academic teaching and publishing, scientists got so used to talking only to other scientists that they inadvertently developed a stylized, ritualistic language that had the unintended effect of shutting out everyone who wasn't yet part of the club.

## Nontraditional Modes of Representation

In part because of a desire and need to broaden the audience for science—particularly in the case of "applied" researchers who have a major interest in having their results communicated to, understood by, and acted upon by nonscientists (either in policy-making circles or among the general public)—it has become more common nowadays for researchers to think in terms of less starchy ways to present their material. It goes without saying that anyone contemplating a career as an academic must still master the traditional form (when academics talk about "publish or perish" they still more often than not mean scholarly monographs, peer-reviewed articles, and presentations at major conferences). But there are now additional ways in which we can reach wider audiences; perhaps as the new modes demonstrate their utility they will come to be as acceptable as the traditional forms when it comes to evaluating the merit of a researcher's activities.

Qualitative research in particular lends itself to less-formal ways of representing data, since it involves narrative descriptions of the lived experience of participants in addition to a statistical summary of their thoughts and behaviors. There are several ways in which this narrative material can be built into the research report. Beginning with alternative representations that are most like the traditional form and ending with those that are the most consciously "creative," they may be described as follows:

- A **realistic** report is one in which extensive quotations from the people who have been interviewed are included in the findings, the better to help the reader "hear" the actual voices of the people whose experiences are being represented. The author of a realistic report is absent, just as he or she would be in a traditional, formal scientific work, but in this case, he or she is concealed behind the words, actions, and ideas of the people he or she has studied, rather than behind a statistical summary of those words, actions, and ideas.

- A **confessional** report is one in which the researcher steps forward and becomes a character is his or her narrative. The act of research is seen as an integral part of the story, particularly in the case of those researchers who believe that their own participation in a community somehow changes what people are doing; the more of a participant a researcher becomes, the more he or she will impact the scene he or she endeavors to describe.

- An **autoethnography** is sometimes described as a "narrative of self." It is a hybrid literary form in which the researcher uses his or her own personal experience as the basis of analysis. The researcher is depicted not as a character in the story of a community, as in a confessional report, but as the case study illuminating a particular issue or theme. Autoethnographies are characterized by dramatic recall, strong metaphors, vivid characters, unusual phrasings, dialogue, and evocative descriptions. The author, however, deliberately withholds interpretation so as to encourage the reader to relive the emotions experienced by the author.

- A **poetic** report is one that weaves the actual words culled from interviews into poetic form. If the study community is one with its own indigenous style of poetry, the researcher will strive to use that style, as well as the words themselves, to capture the worldview of the people. When the same techniques are used to create a dramatic play, the report may be called an *ethnodrama*.

- A **fictional** report is one in which the researcher uses the devices of literary fiction (e.g., the use of composite characters, setting characters in hypothetical events, attributing revelatory interior monologues to people when the researcher could not possibly have heard the original discourse, employing extended metaphors and narrative devices such as flashbacks, flash-forwards, or foreshadowing) to present factual information.

All of these alternative means of presenting the results of research are, like the traditional scientific disquisition, based on the written word. It should be noted, however, that in recent years the "written word" has migrated from its once exclusive home on the printed page to find a place online, on Web sites or blogs of various formats. There are, however, ways to represent research data that rely on other media. Still photography and moving pictures have been a staple of ethnography for decades, but usually as adjuncts to some standard form of the written text. It is becoming increasingly acceptable, however, to use these visual media as the primary means of communicating research results. The visual product has also been presented as a straightforward documentary record; it is now becoming more acceptable to create expressive "fictional" films (analogous to the "fictional" written report described above).

The increasing availability of digital photographic equipment has made it possible to produce high-quality images that can be readily disseminated in ways not possible with traditional photography. It is now possible for researchers to post images (and written text, for that matter) directly on a specially designed Web site. Visual displays have long been a staple of museums or other exhibits, but advances in both photography and graphic design, as well as an increasing acceptance of "creative" (in addition to straight documentary) means of representation, have turned the modern museum or traveling exhibit into an interactive space in which the audience becomes part of the narrative.

## Representing the Sample Project

My choices regarding the final report for this project were clearly limited by the terms to which I had agreed at the outset. For one thing, it was to be an internal document whose primary audience was the hospital administration; dissemination beyond that circle would be strictly up to those in charge. General remarks about the project can be incorporated into other kinds of discussions, such as this book; but there was to be no monograph, journal article, or conference paper that treated the project in any specific detail.

I do not think it would be a breach of the agreement were I to write some sort of fictional report, like a short story. I have used this strategy in other projects in which it was necessary to safeguard the privacy of a "vulnerable" population (e.g., adults with mental retardation who were clients of a community-based habilitation program). In a fictionalized account, I would not have to reveal anyone's identity, since I could create composite characters and change details of the setting and of particular interactions. In doing so, it would be possible to preserve the essence of what I learned at CGH without being too explicit. I have, however, decided not to follow this route, since it would be impossible to fictionalize a large public institution to the extent that it could not be recognized.

So to be faithful to the spirit, not necessarily the letter of my agreement, my final product (the "deliverables," in bureaucratic language) remains a formal, written proprietary report. With the invaluable assistance of one of the hospital's information technology staff members, I was able to include some very nice-looking graphics (e.g., tables, flowcharts, diagrams) that I could not have created nearly as well on my own. Some of those graphics, with accompanying snippets of text, eventually found their way onto the hospital's Web site; I did not, however, have more than a perfunctory say in selecting either the graphics or the text to be placed online. A digest of my findings was included in the orientation program for new hospital staff and volunteers; I was invited to deliver that part of the program myself, although after a while it became more efficient (for the hospital) for me to turn my remarks into a formal script that a hospital employee could deliver without my further input.

I am, for the most part, satisfied that my findings reached their most relevant audience; indeed, it seems very likely that they actually paid attention, as I will discuss in the next chapter. It would be nice to be able to reach a wider audience since the general issue of health care and the social institution of medicine remains a critically important item on the public agenda, but since I knew the limitations on publication going in and accepted them in order to make a contribution to the hospital's evolving corporate culture, I cannot complain. There are, to be sure, cases of researchers who are blindsided by the agencies that support their research; there are also cases of researchers who were so eager to do a piece of research that they failed to establish the terms of agreement in a mutually satisfactory way. But one of the features of doing applied research on behalf of various health and human service agencies is having one's final product treated in a proprietary manner by those agencies. It is an interesting trade-off: one can do independent research for the sake of pure science, and thus have limited impact on public policy; or one can work as a quasi-insider with some (limited) impact on policy but not be able to use the material in the fullest sense as part of the scientific discourse.

## Suggestions for Further Reading

John Van Maanen (1988), *Tales of the Field: On Writing Ethnography* (Chicago: University of Chicago Press); Andrew Sparkes (2002), *Telling Tales in Sport and Physical Activity: A Qualitative Journey* (Champaign, IL: Human Kinetics); Carolyn Ellis and Arthur Bochner, eds. (1996), *Composing Ethnography: Alternative Forms of Qualitative Writing* (Walnut Creek, CA: AltaMira); and Laurel Richardson (1990), *Writing Strategies: Reaching Diverse Audiences* (Newbury Park, CA: Sage) all deal with "creative" alternatives to traditional scientific writing. The unquestioned Bible of traditional style is the *Chicago Manual of Style*, first published in 1906 and currently in its 15th edition (2003) (Chicago: University of Chicago Press); there is now also an online edition. Visual means of representation are treated extensively by Ana Isabel Alfonso, Laszlo Kurti, and Sarah Pink, eds. (2004), *Working Images: Visual Research and Representation in Ethnography* (London: Routledge). Chris Mann and Fiona Stewart (2002) provide a comprehensive overview of research on the Internet in *Internet Communication and Qualitative Research: A Handbook for Researching* (London: Sage). A contemporary look at the theory and practice of designing museums and exhibit spaces is provided by Gail Anderson (2004), *Reinventing the Museum: Historical and Contemporary Perspectives on the Paradigm Shift* (Walnut Creek, CA: AltaMira).

## Questions for Discussion

1. Write up your findings in the form of a standard scientific/academic paper.

2. Select any "alternative" means of representation (written, visual, or online) and translate your scientific paper into that form.

3. Discuss the advantages and disadvantages of both the traditional and the alternative form for the purposes of your particular research project.

# Chapter Nine

# Bringing the Process Full Circle

———◆—◆———

There is an old saying (often attributed to Gandhi, but also to just about every other esteemed moral leader you can think of) to the effect that it is wise to follow the sage who seeks the truth, but folly to follow the one who thinks he's found it. Definitive "truth" is a matter of faith. Science is a matter of inquiry. In science, even the most seemingly settled issues are essentially fodder for further inquiry. How do they know that? What else needs to be learned? What difference does it make?

Since science is a dialogue that does not reach a definitive stopping point, the completion of the eight-step research process brings us to a point where we (or others who are interested in our work) can take the inquiry to its next logical level. With the sharing of your results and your consequent enshrinement as part of "the literature," the process begins anew as you—or other researchers—follow up your leads and formulate research projects of their own (or that they develop in response to a "request for a proposal" published by a funding agency) based on their own eight-step process.

## The Sample Project: Going Forward

Because the project described in this text was "applied" in nature, conducted in response to expressed needs by a public agency that exerted proprietary rights over my findings, my analysis needed to include a set of recommendations for further action. Since my project was not supposed to be evaluative in nature, I had to be very careful, lest any recommendations seem to reflect some sort of negative judgment about ongoing practices and policies at CGH. In other words, based on what I had learned about the evolution of an "ethic of care" at CGH as it was expressed in its pastoral care department and HEC, what suggestions could I offer the hospital administration to enhance the development of this new emphasis in the corporate culture (assuming the administration was indeed serious in wanting to see that development)? Moreover, what still needed to be learned in order to complete the emerging picture of caring at CGH that would made this case study even more relevant to the broader literature on the modern hospital?

I could honestly state in my conclusions that the pastoral care department and HEC at CGH were functioning in appropriate and effective ways. I could further affirm that there were a number of administrative policies in place that confirmed the hospital administration's goal of establishing a culture of caring. Some of those policies reflected government mandates that all hospitals have to follow in order to receive certification (e.g., Joint Commission on the Accreditation of Healthcare Organizations criteria; Medicare and Medicaid laws; provisions of the Health Insurance Portability and Accountability Act;[1] OSHA regulations;[2] ERISA laws;[3] EMTALA standards[4] and Environmental Protection Agency requirements). Other policies were developed with the specific needs of CGH in mind. The main problem for me as a researcher turned out to be something that potentially could be an administrative problem for the hospital—there was, at the time of my study, no coordinating office that oversaw all these efforts. The hospital was caught in the "silo" effect discussed earlier. At the time of the study there was an emerging consensus among hospital administrators nationwide that there needed to be a "corporate compliance officer" who was, in fact, charged with coordinating these efforts. CGH was at the time considering consolidating its policies and procedures under such an officer. I could therefore be asked for my recommendations about how to structure such an office without seeming to criticize a unit or department already in place.

"Corporate compliance" basically means that an institution such as a hospital follows accepted standards and conducts its business in an ethical manner. The broader implication of the term is that the institution is incorporating ethical "care" into its corporate culture, which, in a hierarchical setting such as a hospital, emanates from the administration. A designated Corporate Compliance Officer (CCO) would establish and maintain the hospital's Corporate Code of Conduct, develop compliance-related policies and procedures, establish auditing and monitoring methods to ensure compliance, respond to reported violations, and develop processes to prevent further violations. Perhaps the most important function of the CCO would be to set up and monitor a 24-hour hotline through which violations would be reported and handled.

The external regulations and internal policies comprising the hospital's Corporate Code of Conduct can be summarized as emphasizing the following concerns:

- As part of their orientation, employees are to be familiarized with the Code in general and with the local, state, and federal laws and regulations relevant to their particular jobs.

- The hospital is committed to delivering the highest quality of services available; as such, transfers to other facilities may occasionally be necessary (e.g., when another hospital has specialized units dedicated to the treatment of a particular condition), but only when the patient is stabilized and authorized consent has been obtained.

- Potential biomedical or other ethical conflicts in patient care are to be referred to the HEC.

- Each employee is to be treated fairly and with respect.

- The hospital is to comply with environmental laws and provide information on hazardous substances in the workplace.

- Hospital staff are responsible for the security of any personal property a patient brings to the hospital.

- Patient and other corporate information is to be held in strict confidentiality and cannot be released without explicit patient or administrative approval.

- The hospital staff is responsible for producing accurate and reliable records.

- The hospital is bound to deal with all accrediting agencies in an open, direct, and honest manner.

- Hospital staff are to avoid transactions that might be interpreted as conflicts of interest.

- All potential suppliers/vendors are to be given fair and uniform consideration.

- Employees are not to accept unreasonable business or professional courtesies.

- No hospital funds are to be used to support political candidates, and employees cannot work for candidates during work time.

- "Inducements" (e.g., bribes, kickbacks) are forbidden in cases of patient referrals or corporate purchases.

- Requests for information by government agencies are to be reported immediately to the administration.

- The hospital is committed to observing sound environmental practices.

- Agreements or exchanges of information of an anticompetitive nature are not permitted.

- Employees are prohibited from divulging any information that could influence the sale or purchase of CGH bonds.

- Employees have an affirmative duty to report known or suspected violations of relevant law, regulation, the Corporate Code of Conduct, and other CGH policies via the chain of command, or directly to the CCO.

It was noted earlier that CGH has developed a Patients' Bill of Rights. At the time of the study, a small wallet-sized card with the Bill of Rights was given to every patient upon admission, and poster-sized copies were on display at the nurses' station in each unit. Most patients lost track of the small card in the pile of papers they had to fill out in the Admissions office and rarely thought to ask about it once they got to their room; patients who came to the hospital via the emergency room were not consistently given the card. In my view, the card had difficult-to-read tiny print and was couched in rather opaque legalistic language that most patients would not bother to try to decipher. The posters were printed in both English and Spanish, but the cards were available only in English; patients who did not speak English or Spanish—or who were illiterate— were out of luck. In any case, once patients were in their rooms, it was highly unlikely that they would take a stroll down to the nurses' station to peruse the chart. If the hospital wanted to make patients' rights a centerpiece of its ethic of care, as it said it did, then it would have to make the presentation of those rights more accessible. Doing so, I suggested, should be among the earliest priorities of the CCO. The following key points, stated in straightforward language,[5] should be included in a workable Patients' Bill of Rights.

- You have the right to accurate and easily understood information about your health plan, health care professionals, and health care facilities. If you speak a language other than English or Spanish, have a physical or a mental disability, or just don't understand something, you should ask for help so that you can make informed health care decisions.

- You have a right to choose health care providers who can give you high-quality health care when you need it.

- If you have severe pain, an injury, or sudden illness that makes you believe that your health is in serious danger, you have the right to be screened and stabilized using emergency services. You should be able to use these services whenever and wherever you need them, without needing to wait for authorization and without any financial penalty.

- You have the right to know your treatment options and take part in decisions about your care. Parents, guardians, family members, or others that you select can represent you if you cannot make your own decisions.

- You have a right to considerate, respectful care from your doctors, health plan representatives, and other health care providers that does not discriminate against you.

- You have the right to talk privately with health care providers and to have your health care information protected. You also have the right to read and copy your own medical record. You have the right to ask that your doctor change your record if it is not correct, relevant, or complete.

- You have the right to a fair, fast, and objective review of any complaint you have against your health plan, doctors, hospitals, or other health care personnel. This includes complaints about waiting times, operating hours, the actions of health care personnel, and the adequacy of health care facilities.

The American Hospital Association has replaced its Bill of Rights with a brochure entitled "The Patient Care Partnership," which it recommends to its affiliated hospitals. This publication has the advantage of landing on the "caring" side of the contemporary hospital culture; a "Bill of Rights" might be interpreted as something created by the higher-ups and then "given" to a more or less passive patient population, whereas the notion of a "partnership" makes it seem as if patients can and should take an active role in their own care. The brochure also has the advantage of being written in clearly worded English; it is also available on request in Spanish, Chinese, Arabic, Russian, Tagalog, and Vietnamese. On the other hand, it is a multipage document; not all patients will be in the proper condition to read through and digest it thoroughly. Nevertheless, it provides some important ideas regarding a patient's involvement in his or her own care, points that should be seriously considered as CGH rethinks its own statement:

- To make an informed decision with your doctor, you need to understand: the benefits and risks of the suggested treatment; whether the treatment is experimental or part of a research study; what you can reasonably expect from your treatment, and any long-term effects it might have on your quality of life; what you and your family will need to do after you leave the hospital; the financial consequences of using uncovered services or out-of-network providers.

- You, in turn, need to give your caregivers complete and correct information about your health and coverage, such as: past illnesses, surgeries, or hospitalizations; past allergic reactions; any medicines or dietary supplements (such as vitamins and herbs) that you are taking; any network or admission requirements under your health plan.

- You also have a right to inform your health care providers about any goals, values, or spiritual beliefs that are important to your well-being.

- If you have signed a health care power of attorney stating who should speak for you if you become unable to make decisions for yourself, or if you have signed a "living will" or "advance directive" that states your wishes about end-of-life care, give copies to your doctor, your family, and other members of your care team. If you or your spokesperson need help preparing these documents, counselors, social workers, and/or chaplains should be available to you.

- The confidentiality of your relationship with your doctor and the privacy of your records will be strictly maintained. You have a right to request a copy of information from the hospital's records about your care.

- Hospital staff will file claims for you with your health insurers or other programs such as Medicare and Medicaid. They will also help your doctor with needed documentation. If you do not have health insurance, the hospital will try to help you and your family find financial assistance or make other arrangements.

In terms of research, it seems that the next logical step would be to conduct an inquiry based in the office of the Corporate Compliance Officer; it would be advantageous to begin as soon as possible, as the office is getting organized, and follow it as it develops its policies and procedures. Like the project that yielded these findings, this new project would be based on the analysis of archived documents (*not*, of course, including patient records) and interviews with the staff of the compliance office. Observations of actions taken to monitor compliance (e.g., accreditation visitations, responses to hotline tips) would also be included, although I would not be as much of a "participant" observer as I was when I could function as a chaplain intern while observing the pastoral care department. Given the growing literature on corporate compliance in the hospital sector, it would be important to produce a detailed case study that could compare and contrast with trends recorded nationally. Conducting an ethnographic study of a corporate bureaucracy would represent very new territory for me, but I realize that this would be a relatively difficult baton to pass along, since no other outside qualitative researcher currently enjoys the same established entrée at CGH. It thus represents a challenge as well as an opportunity for me as an applied social researcher.

And so the process of inquiry continues . . .

## SUGGESTIONS FOR FURTHER READING

The masochists among you who yearn to become conversant with hospital bureaucracy might want to check out Debbie Troklus and Greg Warner (2009), *Compliance 101* (Minneapolis: Health Care Compliance Association), the definitive guidebook by the main professional association in the field; it tells you everything you have been longing to know about the fundamentals of health care compliance.

## QUESTIONS FOR DISCUSSION

1. Write a brief essay in which you sketch some tentative plans to follow up the research project you have just completed.

OR

Write a brief essay in which you outline some aspects of your research project that you would like to see some other researcher follow up on.

2. In a group with other members of your class and your instructor, discuss the three most important things you have learned by following this research process.

# NOTES

[1] HIPAA, among other things, is concerned with the security and privacy of health data.

[2] The Occupational Safety and Health Administration is concerned with the on-the-job well-being of workers.

[3] The Employee Retirement Income Security Act is a one of a body of laws (generically referred to as ERISA) regulating employee benefit plans.

[4] The Emergency Medical Treatment and Active Labor Act requires hospitals and ambulance services to provide care to anyone needing emergency treatment regardless of citizenship, legal status, or ability to pay.

[5] This outline was adapted from a statement issued by the American Cancer Society (ACS). Various other health advocacy groups have created Bills of Rights of their own, but the ACS statement struck me as being among the most clearly and succinctly written.

# Index